'This book is packed with ideas from an author combining the e:
parish priest and educationalist with passionate commitment to .
at the heart of worship. The style is easy and the ideas often simple – but Sandra
is a shrewd observer of contemporary culture and gives us imaginative options for
worship today.'

The Revd Sally Davenport, Priest-in-Charge, Holy Trinity with St Columba, Fareham

'It's refreshing to have a practical book on all-age worship which doesn't assume
that all churches have large numbers of children, access to technology and flexible
spaces! This book will be useful to the tiny Norman village church as well as the
flourishing suburban congregation – and all churches in between! A welcome
addition to any worship leader's resource shelf.'

Mary Hawes, National Children's Adviser, Church of England

Also available:

Festivals Together: Creating all-age worship through the year

Worship
Together

Creating all-age services that work

December · January · February · March · April · May · June · July · August · September · October · November

SANDRA MILLAR

First published in Great Britain in 2012

Society for Promoting Christian Knowledge
36 Causton Street
London SW1P 4ST
www.spckpublishing.co.uk

British Library Cataloguing-in-Publication Data
A catalogue record for this book is available from the British Library

ISBN 978–0–281–06629–2
eBook ISBN 978–0–281–06630–8

Typeset by Graphicraft Ltd, Hong Kong
First printed in Great Britain by Ashford Colour Press
Subsequently digitally printed in Great Britain

Produced on paper from sustainable forests

For Ben and Suzy, simply my favourite young people

Contents

Acknowledgements

The author would like to thank all the children and adults who have so willingly engaged with worship and shared their thoughts.

The author and publisher would also like to thank those who read and commented on the text.

Introduction

As the people approach, the streets become more and more crowded. Men are walking along with their sons close by, grandfathers chat with each other and boys run and jump. The women are coming too, some with babies strapped to their backs, toddlers clutching at their skirts. Girls are laughing together and the older generation are being helped along. The noise is tremendous as they gather at their destination. Some people begin to play musical instruments, banging drums and waving tambourines. Voices are raised in song and some women begin to dance. There is lots of laughter and talking, before a murmur goes through the crowd. A great shout goes up, a shout of joy and praise. All the people shout back and the worship begins.

Imagining worship in the days of Moses and the prophets is difficult. But one thing we do know is that it seems everyone was present (see, for example, Nehemiah 12.43). The instruction is explicit – men, women and children are called to attend. When the book of the law is read (2 Kings 23.1–3) everyone who is able to understand needs to be there. In Hebrew the word for child (*tassim*) implies almost any age from around 4 years old, the age at which a child could begin helping with basic chores, and could use language to respond.

It is not only on happy occasions but also at times of repentance and sorrow that everyone gathers. The prophet Joel specifically calls everyone – men, women, children and infants – to repent and proclaim a solemn fast (Joel 2.16). Travel forward to the early Church, and once more we have households of faith gathering to break bread and wine, to listen to Peter or Paul (Acts 20.7–12) speak, to offer songs and prayers together. In that time and place, children were simply present to what was happening – all the people were joined in worship.

The challenge of all-age worship

Over the years I have asked myself many times how this 'gathering of everyone' can possibly happen. If everyone is meant to be included in worship, how come it's so very difficult? For the Church has certainly struggled with this idea in recent generations. As our culture has developed an increased understanding of children, separating them into narrower developmental stages, so it seems to have become more and more difficult to bring children, young people and adults together to worship in music, word and sacrament. We have special programmes for under-2s, for preschoolers, for sixes to eights and nines to elevens, and teenagers are always a distinct category. At training events, I often invite people to make a human scale where 10 represents the view 'I love all-age worship and can't get enough' and 1 'This is the worst Sunday of the month'. Generally, people cluster in the lower half of the scale – with the occasional inspired person admitting to thinking all-age worship is fantastic.

All sorts of reasons are wheeled out: children can't concentrate; the noise they make disturbs people; adults need something that is challenging; action songs are irritating; it takes too long to prepare. These, and many variations upon them, are offered as reasons why we are so uncomfortable with the concept of everyone worshipping together.

The all-age experience: clues from culture

Imagine another scene. The streets are filling up with people making their way to the venue. Men and women walk along with their friends, pushing buggies, holding the hands of younger ones. Granddads are chatting excitedly with their grandchildren, and Grandma is helping with the baby. There is a palpable air of excitement. As the venue fills up, people begin singing and cheering, laughter breaks out, until the moment comes when the whistle blows, and the match begins.

Rugby football is an amazingly all-age activity. On a home Saturday in Gloucester I watch the fans converging on the stadium, and it is a truly multi-generational experience. On closer conversation with some of these families, I discover the absolute importance of taking children to the match. I discover the excitement with which Dad, Mum, grandparents, aunts, uncles and friends approach each game. I learn that the first match at which a child is able to understand (not the first they may have attended – some go as toddlers in pushchairs or babes in slings) is a real thrill for the older generation. Adults long to explain things and share their enthusiasm. The atmosphere is great.

This all-age event makes no concession to the presence of children. The match time remains at 45 minutes each half. The rules are not simplified. The children are not taken off to a special 'learn about rugby' session (although there are lots of opportunities for children to play rugby with their peers at other times). There are other sports with the same kind of multi-generational approach: an expectation that everyone who is there is going to have an experience, whether joyful or sorrowful, exciting or dull, and find memories that will stay with them over the years.

> An expectation that everyone who is there is going to have an experience, whether joyful or sorrowful, exciting or dull, and find memories that will stay with them over the years

There are many more things in our culture that speak across generations: an outing to a science museum, a visit to the ballet *The Nutcracker* or a performance of Handel's *Messiah*, for example. Again, no concessions are made to children. The conductor doesn't suddenly decide to miss out all the quiet bits, and introduce actions to help the children understand. Something else is happening – adults are passing on their passionate conviction that this event matters. They long for the children to discover the delight that they have discovered in music, dance or sport. Their enthusiasm is contagious and they are the ones who whisper explanations and encouragement as the event unfolds. Arms go round children and fingers point out details, questions are answered and as children notice and discover aspects of the event, parents are really pleased.

Let's move for a moment to the cinema. Children are very excited, and parents are pretty relaxed as they go in to the big screen. They are going to see the latest family-friendly film from Pixar or a similar company. The children, some as young as 3, are laughing at the bright colours and entranced by the story. The older children laugh at much of the humour and fall silent in moments of tension. Sometimes there is an outburst of laughter from the adults at parts of the script only intended for them. It's an all-age experience. In fact, when I went to watch *Toy Story 3* there were no children in the audience at all – and lots of very adult weeping – which tells us something about how effective these movies are at communicating with all-ages. The typical length of these films is 90 minutes, although some are much longer, and there is no doubt that the vast majority of children can concentrate throughout, apart from the occasional 'comfort' break.

Disney is also master of all-age, cross-generational communication. A few years ago I decided to celebrate a significant birthday by going to Disneyland Paris with my sister and her children. We had a fantastic time. Sometimes all of us went on rides, sometimes just two of us. There were things for the children to do without the adults – and places where only adults went. As we travelled home we reflected together and decided we couldn't think of much else that we could have done together so effectively. It may surprise you to learn that the children were aged 15 and 21 years old! Somehow it was perfectly acceptable to be a family of our shape, of our ages and everywhere we looked there were multi-generational families enjoying themselves. Christians may wish to critique the Disney world view, but as an all-age experience it also has much to show us as we seek to develop effective worship for everyone.

What is worship?

Worship is at the heart of our Christian lives. It is not an optional extra, but is something we have been created to do, as succinctly stated in the Westminster Shorter Catechism of 1647: 'The chief end of man (*sic*) is to glorify God, and to enjoy him for ever.' This purpose is deeply embedded in Scripture, throughout the law (in Exodus or Leviticus) and the prophets, as well as explicitly in the Psalms and other praise songs (for example, Psalms 66, 84, 92, 150).

Worship is something that first takes place in our daily Christian living as we encounter God through creation, circumstance, human beings, culture and in the intimate spaces of our own thoughts. Worship can burst from us in shouts of praise, in litanies of thanksgiving and in silent adoration. Sometimes it is expressed or communicated through sublime music, a perfect sentence or the brilliant fluidity of human movement. The amazing thing is that this incredibly profound personal experience is also capable of being experienced when we gather together as the people of God. It might be in a crowd of 20,000 young people from across the world singing together of God's power and glory, or in the more intimate experience of three adults sharing words from 400 years ago in the dim light of a country church. Worship is both personal and corporate, both mind-stretching and the simplest of things. It is this profound activity that is the purpose of gathering together, for some in the discipline of the daily offices, for many in the weekly form of the Sunday service.

> **Worship is both personal and corporate, both mind-stretching and the simplest of things**

Worship is not something we discover as adults: the impulse to give glory to God is there when the toddler starts dancing to the hymns or when the 9-year-olds roar their praise shout. It is there when children are alone, as when my nephew, aged 5, stood still in the centre of a field of waving corn and cried – 'Oh God, thank you for your amazing world!' as he turned slowly in a circle. And it is there when they gather together, as at Spring Harvest when a thousand eights to elevens fell silent as we thought about God's great love for each of us.

Children in worship

In recent decades, there has been an emerging understand of children as spiritual beings.

Theologians have begun to reflect seriously on the meaning of childhood at the same time as psychologists, Christian and others, have researched the minds and thoughts of children in relation to spiritual matters (see p. 101 for Recommended reading).

> **Those who engage with children often know that they are capable of deep insight and response**

Those who engage with children often know that they are capable of deep insight and response. So what happens when they come to church, to a gathering of the people of God?

'All-age' worship is a strange phrase. It is strange because although the meaning would seem to be self-evident, in reality something odd happens as the words move from one person's lips into another's mind. When I say 'all-age', others often hear the word 'children'. The word 'family' in this context is no better: if someone asks me if I have any family, I invariably reply that nowadays it is very small – a sister and her children plus a vast array of cousins. I know that what they are really asking is whether I have any children of my household or my body. 'How's the family?' is invariably an enquiry about offspring. So when we announce that a service is 'all-age' or 'family' worship, we run the risk of it being seen as aimed at children alone.

There are many things in our lives and in our culture that are intended solely for children. For example, visiting the splash pool at the leisure centre or watching *Teletubbies* or *Postman Pat*. When adults sit down to do or watch these things with their children it is for the vicarious pleasure that comes from watching them laugh with delight and singing along to the happy tunes. There is absolutely no expectation that the content will stimulate adult reflection, take one into a deeper insight into life or give an answer to a current moral dilemma. The criteria for the success of the programme is that the children are occupied, quiet and still for a block of time!

There are media and activities for older children that do engage adults very well, but often these serve to remind us that children are much more sophisticated than we give them credit for. I watched a programme recently in which the presenter explored his fear of water. He went to a series of places with a psychologist, engaged in experiences, talked openly about his feelings and eventually moved towards overcoming his fear. The programme? *Blue Peter*, a programme with a target audience of 6- to 11-year-olds. It is possible for adults to engage with good children's events, but it happens more as a by-product rather than intentionally.

The problem with much of the worship termed 'all-age' in our churches is that it is not of the calibre of *Blue Peter*. Instead it is aimed at the younger child, and adults have little expectation that they will be engaged, let alone challenged. They are not there to worship – they are there to watch. If that is what is intended, then call it a children's service. In this type of service, the children hand out books, do the readings, say the prayers and come forward for a special blessing. The parents are happy – but it is definitely not all-age worship.

Multi-generational worship?

There is another term we could use which is much more descriptive, but sadly not very usable. In the USA I learned about multi-generational worship, worship which is accessible to people at different ages and stages. This is the real heart of what we call all-age worship. It is about creating worship that offers the possibility of an encounter with the living God for whoever is present. Sometimes churches spend hours preparing an elaborate and complex 'family service', only to find that on Sunday morning there are only two children present – and they are the churchwarden's grandchildren, staying for the weekend. Everyone is downcast and the result is that the adults present have to pretend to be children for the morning – which they may or may not enjoy. Conversely, we have the experience of walking in to a normal parish Eucharist and finding two young families present, and then spend the first 10 minutes apologizing to them for the lack of provision.

> All-age, multi-generational worship should be able to appeal to a wide cross-section of people

All-age, multi-generational worship should be able to appeal to a wide cross-section of people. It should be possible for the church to enable people to come together, across the age ranges, and for each one of them to go away knowing that they have met with God and given glory to his name.

So I started to look at Disney, Pixar, rugby football and a whole host of activities which successfully communicate with all generations. I think it's possible for the Church to do what is normative in our culture and was so much a part of biblical life. I know that many will point out that the resources available to Disney, Pixar and Gloucester RFC are infinitely greater than the resources available to the tiny church in Upper Snodbury-in-the-Grass or the struggling inner-city community. Financially, that may be the case. But what is achieved in the films and events does not begin with the money. It begins with the creativity of human beings and their desire to communicate effectively and offer something that is worthwhile to all ages. God didn't give all the best ideas to those employed by the big corporations of the world! Every human is made in the image of God and therefore has the capacity for creativity, relationship and imagination among other things. The Church needs to become more confident in its ability to communicate effectively with all ages, and to begin to use the gifts present in its midst, regardless of technological and financial resources.

Respecting difference

All-age communication begins with the desire to make relationships. Corporate worship is also about relationship – with one another and with God. It needs to reflect the diversity of the people of God who are together and individually on their journey of faith and life. It should be dynamic and transformative, reflecting the way in which the church community is moving in its discipleship and mission. Even the most apparently static church is changing, for the way we are formed

> Even the most apparently static church is changing, for the way we are formed as human beings is intrinsically about change

as human beings is intrinsically about change. There are absolutely obvious differences between a baby and an 18-year-old, between a 25-year-old and a

65-year-old; throughout our lives we change physically, emotionally and intellectually. The challenge in creating and leading all-age worship is to be mindful of the differences and yet be aware that at every stage people are in relationship with God.

Babies in arms need primarily to experience corporate worship as a place of safety, where they can still be confident their basic needs are being met by their primary caregivers. The task of a congregation is to reflect God's calm accepting love of each infant, and the Creator's delight in their presence. Sadly, the first thing most babies hear on arriving in church is 'Sshhh'. The parents are tense because they are coming into church where they are uncertain of their welcome and that sets up an uncertainty in the child – who responds by crying. If all-age worship is really for everyone, congregations need to think about how they respond to babies and how they can help parents feel supported and accepted.

Toddlers are energetic explorers. Every single thing in the world is a source of wonder as anyone who has tried to walk 50 metres with a newly mobile infant knows. These children are discovering the world, finding out about their own bodies and the environment they inhabit. They learn about hard and soft – the contrast between cushions and floor; about high and low, as they crawl under a table and try to stand up; about the taste of sand and the taste of ice cream. There is so much going on in the early years – and this is how God has created human beings. As a species we need more support and encouragement to be able to grow in confidence than any other, so an 18-month-old crawling in the nave is not naughty but normal! For children of this age, life is a multi-sensory experience.

This continues throughout early childhood, as children develop an increasing range of skills including language and movement. Slowly their world expands as they discover a wider circle of relationships. Younger children experience a whole range of emotions, and have a vast inner world of imaginative possibilities. Wonder is part of life!

Older children have different needs. They are all about thinking and doing, needing to engage mind and body and not worry too much about the consequences. The age group most likely to end up in casualty are 7- to 11-year-olds as they fearlessly plan and plot their adventures. They need responsibility and challenge, opportunities to exercise their brains and their bodies as they continue to explore the world they live in. Whereas a 5-year-old is awed by the beauty of creation, an 8-year-old wants to know how it works – and the more gruesome the detail the better! The Horrible Histories series of books is written with this age group firmly in mind.

Once a child reaches the age of puberty, somewhere between 11 and 14, so much changes. Developmentally, the locus of relationship widens significantly and friends become equal to family in significance, at times even more so. Awareness of how other people might think about us develops, with huge consequences for self-confidence and belonging. But there is also a growing knowledge about the world and a developing range of skills and interests which need affirming and encouraging. Teenagers are arguably the most difficult group to engage in 'all-age worship'. Developmentally, they are inclined towards gatherings of their peer group, rather than family gatherings. Churches simply need to welcome them with gladness, rejoice that they participate (rather than moaning that they only turn up when they have a job to do or arrive seconds before the start), and allow them space to be themselves. Time passes, and then of course, we continue to change and develop through young adulthood and on through the years.

Church as a household of faith

This is how God designed human beings – so that we would be different at every stage of life. No wonder it seems so difficult to gather this diversity together! Yet that is the challenge of all-age, multi-generational worship which will enable all those present to encounter God. The model we have to build on is the family or household of faith. Thinking about our church as a household is often a significant shift in the way we relate to different generations and the expectations we have. Without even realizing it consciously, church slips into a way of being which is more like a shared-interest club, where families are welcome sometimes.

When I was a child we used to visit a working men's club on a Saturday night when there were special family events. It was very exciting because I knew that the rest of the time we weren't allowed in at all. I had stood in the doorway from time to time while my dad and his mates chatted at the bar. I knew we were there as a treat – and we had to behave properly or we would be sent away. The club was set up for adults to meet adult needs. There is nothing wrong with this at all. But it is not what the local church is supposed to be.

In contrast there is family life with all its give and take. During a typical family week there will be times when the children have priority, and time for adults, but also a great deal of time when everyone simply goes about life together. We don't have to think consciously about whether the children should be with us in the house on Saturday mornings – they are just there. In my multi-cultural neighbourhood there are lots of multi-generational households, where there is an easy exchange of roles and responsibilities and all find a place to belong together. Church is a household of faith, a family of God's people. There will be times when we need to meet with our peers to learn and to share, but those times are the exception. The starting point is that everyone simply belongs and normal behaviour is that we do things together. This will include social and work activities, plans for the future as well as worship. If a family decides to make alterations to its home, it's usual to think about the impact on the children, and if they

> The starting point is that everyone simply belongs and normal behaviour is that we do things together

are old enough (probably 3 or 4 upwards) to tell them what is happening and invite them in on appropriate decisions. At the very least we tell them what is going on. But in church we forget that children are part of the family, and we easily forget to include them in our plans.

Key components of all-age worship

At every stage of development, people are growing in their relationship with God and God's people. This happens in our home life, in our community life, in our church life and it needs to spill over into our worship. But how can we hold such diverse needs together? After much time looking at a wide range of events and activities that work well for all ages together I have identified some key characteristics, and this book explores how we can build those characteristics more effectively into our worship. The good news is that many of them are already intrinsic to our worship: we simply need to be more aware of how effective they might be when the range of those who are worshipping widens to include different generations.

The first characteristic is **structure and repetition**. Families like returning to activities because they find a framework which they can trust. Children feel safe and grow in confidence when they know what is happening, and then when the unexpected happens we all experience that together. Disorganized and haphazard activities create uncertainty. It may look like fun to be running amok but as any book or programme on childcare will tell you it is only fun when there is a deep security underlying it. **Chapter 1** looks at the basic structure of all our worship gatherings and explores ideas for building a strong framework that can be used as the basis for every service.

Second, all-age activities are **multi-sensory**, working on multiple levels simultaneously. Children and adults are engaged through visual stimuli, words, movement and a whole range of other sensory activities. Some of them work in a very direct way for younger children, others will speak to adults. **Chapter 2** looks at how we can use the space in our churches more effectively, and include activities in worship that use the senses and the body in ways that help everyone present to engage in worship.

One of the surprising characteristics of all-age activities is the way in which **mystery and wonder** are integral. Children are constantly being open to moments of surprise and astonishment which can be shared with the multi-generations around them. Together families discover the delights of an under-water world at the aquarium; together they experience the semi-darkness of the reptile house at the zoo or the contrast between light and dark in the rides at the theme park. **Chapter 3** looks at how we can build on the deepest mystery and wonder that lies at the heart of our Christian faith. It also explores how the Eucharist should be a service of inclusion and a real expression of multi-generational worship for everyone present rather than being seen as something reserved for grown-ups.

Perhaps the most significant strength in all-age activities is **story**, not just the direct telling of stories but the potential to be engaged in an unfolding story and to build that into the story of our own lives. Being part of the crowd at the rugby match is engaging with the story of the team and the fans. There are also more direct stories that need to be told, that speak across centuries and down generations. **Chapter 4** explores the universal themes that lie at the heart of such stories, and looks at how we can incorporate them into worship, and particularly into the talk, in all-age services.

Finally, **Chapter 5** offers some ideas and practical tips for **leading a service**. It suggests that multi-generational worship is the responsibility of the whole congregation, as well as the worship leaders. There are ideas for involving a wide spread of ages and practical suggestions about preparing and planning, plus some guidelines about how to use the outlines in this book.

Part 2 includes 12 all-age worship outlines. These are designed to be used in the simplest of church settings. They are not dependent on the presence of children, the availability of a screen and technology, or access to a worship band – although all of these are valuable. There are services for each month of the year, giving churches a chance to do something for everyone on any Sunday in the year.

However all of these are simply tools. Imagine again a Sunday morning as a family make their way to church. Imagine them approaching with the same enthusiasm as the crowd going to the rugby match as parents share their expectation that church is a good thing, in fact, the most important and exciting thing ever. Imagine the church family members sitting alongside the children, pointing out things of interest, whispering explanations, sharing amazement as children encounter God through the building, the words, the music and the people. My hope is that this will become a reality in your church as you discover how to create worship for everyone present. Enjoy the journey!

> Worship needs to be good enough to engage and delight all the children of God whether 8 or 80. Boring worship is an affront to God, let alone a turn-off to the assembly.[1]

Note

1 Richard Giles, *At Heaven's Gate*, Norwich: Canterbury Press, 2010, p. 25.

Part 1

Creating all-age worship: the key components

1

Skeletons and shapes

When my niece was about 4 years old I took her with me to a mid-week Book of Common Prayer Eucharist in the market-town Anglican church near where she lived. She was at the age when doing anything with a visiting auntie seems exciting. She was accustomed to churchgoing of a different kind in a nonconformist chapel, but I thought it would round out her spiritual formation to include her Church of England heritage. She sat modestly through the service paying attention, until we came to the Lord's Prayer when she suddenly clutched at my sleeve and whispered in a dramatic undertone: 'They're saying our prayer!' Suddenly she could join in and belong.

It's important for all of us to be able to join in. Shared rituals make us feel included – think about the importance of chants at football matches or the gathering at the beginning of a Brownie meeting. Almost everyone knows how the TV programme *Strictly Come Dancing* begins – with an invitation and response. 'Nice to see you,' says Brucie and we all chorus: 'To see you, nice' and we know where we are. The programme then follows a very set pattern until the closing exhortation to 'keep dancing'. This structure and the repeated phrases are accessible to all ages, from toddlers to great-grannies. People don't need books or instruction: we can relax into the safety net of the structure, and then when the unexpected happens we all share in the sense of uncertainty or enjoyment.

Ask almost any adult of a certain age if they can remember the shapes of the windows of the children's programme *Playschool* and a chorus of 'round, square, arched' will come back without a pause for breath. The windows never changed,

except for one brief period of experimentation with new shapes – but viewers found this so unsettling that the old shapes were quickly brought back. You could be sure that there wouldn't be the sudden appearance of a dodecahedron or a rhomboid or even a simple triangle. The structure was in place – going through the windows then opened up all sorts of experiences and possibilities.

Structure is the foundation of all our worship, whether designed for all ages or for a specific purpose. In many churches we are so used to structure we forget that it's there – it's a bit like the skeleton of our human bodies. Without a skeleton we wouldn't be able to move, run, dance, write, speak. But until it goes wrong few of us give it a second thought during an average day or year.

> Structure is the foundation of all our worship, whether designed for all ages or for a specific purpose

'Family worship' often makes us aware of the skeleton, the structure, in ways that make us uncomfortable or insecure. Some kinds of worship seem to dispense with the structure altogether – the skeleton is taken away and instead we have a free-form flow of action songs, drama, games, most of which is aimed at entertaining 6-year-olds and ends up with a whole lot of overexcited toddlers and some stunned adults. I know this is overstating the case but it really happens.

The structure of all-age worship

The basic structure of all worship gatherings is the same. It consists of four stages, with two subsets.

It doesn't matter whether it's a music-led informal 'worship' service or a formal wedding, this basic shape creates flow, builds cohesion and helps worshippers of all ages to find their way into the space where they can encounter God. This basic shape is:

- We gather
- We listen
- We respond
- We go out.

The two subsets are saying sorry and celebration (in bread and wine). This remains the shape, even when the central two phases are more flexible. For example, it is sometimes appropriate to split the listen and response parts into two or more sections: gather, listen, respond, listen, respond, listen, respond, go out. The music, prayers, readings, movements and activities become the contents within each of these phases – the revelation through the window, as it were. Each section has its own distinctive purpose in the overall structure.

WE GATHER

Whatever the occasion there has to be some sense of having created a special or significant space. It might be as informal as the moment a guitar chord is struck or as formal as the words which begin a marriage service: 'Dearly beloved, we are gathered here today', but it is always about creating the sense that we are together as a group, gathered for a purpose.

The purpose of the gathering is twofold. First it encloses the time and space, setting it aside for a purpose. This is exactly what happens at the beginning of other gatherings – as in the Brownie meeting as the children gather around the toadstool or at the beginning of a Women's Institute meeting when the president calls order. Second it draws all those present into a shared sense of purpose, often explicitly stating that purpose. All-age worship needs this same process of gathering to help include everyone within the space, and, where appropriate, to reflect the specifics of the day, whether that is a church celebration, theological idea or something that has happened in the community or the wider world.

✔ Tip

One of the most basic forms of introduction is: 'The Lord be with you.'

Response And also with you.

This is a fantastic opening for all ages. Both invitation and response are simple: the response is only four words and can quickly be learned by even the youngest child. If it stays the same every time, children will soon realize that it signals the time for beginning and the time for worship. There are lots of other effective ways of doing this – lighting candles, greeting each other, etc. But probably the most important thing is consistency so that there is a clear signpost and sense of belonging.

The basic greeting can then be followed by informal and friendly words of welcome, with allusions to the day, the place, the time, topical events, etc. (The chapter on leading includes tips on how to do this well, and the importance of smiling!) Although *Common Worship* suggests this as one of the times when notices are appropriate, they may well be more relevant later in the service, so that the opening focus stays with worship. Commonly a hymn or song follows – there is a wealth of books and resources on children and all-age songs but lots of them depend on two key factors:

- lots of children and
- accomplished musicians.

You may have neither, but bear in mind that this is not about creating for children alone, but for whoever is present.

✔ Tip

It is a good idea to use well-known hymns and tunes, especially for the opening song. This enables people to feel confident about joining in and creates a sense of belonging – remember the singing before the rugby match! Providing instruments can also be helpful – encourage all ages to try them out rather than just giving them to the children. This will avoid creating a sense of 'childishness' and also might help to keep the accompaniment tuneful.

If you are creating a eucharistic service you may want to include some kind of opening activity or response that would replace the 'Prayer of preparation' in *Common Worship* and help to set the theme. If you look at the March liturgy, for example, you will see an invitation and response which helps people to think about journeying (see p. 55).

It is important that invitations and responses are inclusive.

(see p. 55)

✔ Tip

Ask the question: 'If someone can't read, how can they join in?' Putting words on screens does not always increase inclusivity, although it might well help some and it does help to increase the sound level as heads are lifted up and words spoken to the ceiling rather than the floor!

However, many of our churches cannot access technology, either because of the costs or the style of the building or simply because it is not appropriate. Using the method developed over centuries of a 'cantor' or lead voice with response is often very successful with all ages.

Praying together is also vital, and the gathering part of the service ends with a 'collect' or prayer for the day, which is usually led by a minister. This is an opportunity for everyone to become still for a moment and listen to the words of the prayer, making them their own as they join in with the 'Amen'.

We say sorry

This subset of the basic shape is very flexible – it often appears early in the service as part of the gathering, but alternatively can become part of a response to the word. But it is so flexible that it's often missed out altogether in family-style worship when Communion is not being celebrated, which is a great shame. The space for penitence allows for reflection and gives space to acknowledge the hurts that people of all ages bring with them to a gathering. Children are very familiar with failure and disappointment. Hardly a day goes by for most 7- to 10-year-olds without something, somewhere, going wrong. They may fall out with friends, disappoint teachers, disobey parents.

Saying sorry and making reparation is part of their life experience, so to ignore this in church seems strange. There is also a sense in which penitence becomes a space to acknowledge the wrong that exists in the world in a general sense, and the harm that others may have done to us.

Children may also bring sorrow and hurt with them to church. Many are only too aware of the anger and pain of adults close to them. All of this needs time to be acknowledged. Penitence can sometimes be reframed as lament – a sense of sorrow as we remember together all that is wrong in God's world. In a Mothering Sunday service we invited everyone to come forward and place a stone on the altar in response to a series of statements with *kyrie* ('Lord, have mercy') responses which included recalling those who cannot have children, and those who are separated from the children or parents they love. The effect was profound. As all ages moved to the front, there were tears shed and hands held with a very real sense of God's presence.

✔ Tip

We do not need to avoid stillness or quiet when children are present – we simply need to help them enter and exit such times with expectation.

WE LISTEN
This brings us to the core of the structure. This is when we hear God's word through the reading of Scripture and explanation in a sermon or talk. It is this that will provoke our response in prayer and celebration. It is common in all-age services to limit the readings to just one, which must be the Gospel reading if the service is a Eucharist, but it is possible to include more readings as long as they are presented well. There are creative suggestions in the outlines for presenting the readings, and it may be appropriate to use a variety of approaches if there are two or more readings, such as a drama and a straightforward reading from a contemporary translation (for example, see the outline for June, p. 70). If the all-age service is truly to be worship for everyone present, happening every week, then it is

(for example, see the outline for June, p. 70)

important to make sure that the content also has the potential to engage everyone. The lectionary is a great blessing as well as a great challenge to those of us preparing all-age worship, but using it as the basis for teaching and worship themes helps to ensure that we present a breadth of biblical stories and Christian doctrines, rather than concentrating on the old favourites that we think are suitable for children. It seems a lot easier to build a service around the story of the Good Samaritan rather than that of the Syro-Phoenician woman or to talk about David and Goliath rather than the prophecies of Isaiah or Amos. But presented and explored well all of this material is appropriate for all ages.

Listening to the readings or to the sermon is not about everybody present being able to engage equally with everything that is said. Those of us who are involved in preaching on a regular basis know that for every sermon preached there are 20 or more different sermons heard – and sometimes people hear things that we know we didn't say! The words take root and make links with people's experiences and concerns in unique ways, and as minds wander and ruminate around the things that are happening so the word of God becomes alive and active.

Children are the same – they respond to different, sometimes unexpected, parts of the word and exploration. Or it may be that for them listening is also about noticing. An Epiphany carol service held each year at Tewkesbury Abbey in Gloucestershire is attended by hundreds, including lots of children and infants. The service is highly formal with carols, readings and choral pieces. It also features incense, processions and movement. One year, I sat behind a family with three children. The older two stood on chairs to see, moved out into the aisle at key moments, and eagerly joined in with candle-lighting. The youngest, aged around 3, simply lay on his back across a couple of seats and gazed up into the darkened cavern of the abbey, into the mysterious and beautiful space of the nave and ceiling. His listening was about noticing, about being in the space and letting words flow around him.

Much of our liturgy and worship has become overly dependent on words. We judge success in terms of understanding, whereas worship should be about an experience of relationship with God and God's people which happens both with and beyond language.

✔ Tip

Listening might include the visual stimuli offered by our worship space as well as by intentionally introduced images, which might be two- or three-dimensional.

Many churches have begun to introduce ways of exploring the Christian story by creating stations or tableaux which interpret biblical texts. Schoolchildren are invited to discover the story in fresh ways through these encounters, and yet when we invite the same children into church for a worship service, we all too frequently produce a static, word-based delivery. It is possible to 'listen' to the word being presented not just through drama and text but through visually exciting interactive installations.

Music can also be an important part of listening. An all-age worship gathering often includes those who are on the fringe of church, or who may be attending after a long absence since their own childhood.

✔ Tip

Singing can be an embarrassing and alien activity, making people feel awkward and excluded. Listening to music is a much more comfortable and familiar activity in today's culture, and it may sometimes be appropriate to listen together to a piece of music, which might be sacred or secular. This means being aware of music popular with all ages – for example, the X Factor winning song or a contemporary boy band may be known to both children and grandparents.

Recorded music is also a good way of introducing new material, which might later be sung in worship.

WE RESPOND

Responding to worship can take many different forms. It might involve music, singing, words, silence or activity. However, for most traditional churches there are some things that feature regularly, beginning with prayer. Intercessory prayer is one of the great joys of traditional worship, encouraging all God's people to think beyond themselves and to bring the concerns of the world, the Church and those they love to God.

One day I was walking along the road near where I live when I met two girls on their way to school. They stopped to admire my dog (he's very used to it!), and then the older girl, who was aged about 10, began to talk to me. There was a large puddle, so large it might even be called a mini-flood, at the end of the road. She pointed towards it and made some comment about it being a problem. I nodded in agreement, but then she veered off in a new direction. 'It's not as bad as Mozambique though,' she said in a slightly belligerent, admonishing tone. I must have looked a bit surprised. She talked a bit more about floods in Mozambique and how people's lives are affected before adding, 'I watch a lot of news, you know.' We parted, she and her sister to school, me to ponder how we constantly underestimate and undervalue children's knowledge, experience and interests. I live in a deprived urban area – a long way from affluent, educated middle England. I imagined this girl going off to church, only to be offered 'If I were a butterfly' in response to her deep concerns about the world.

I have also had conversations with children about the ethics of euthanasia, about structural sin and about homelessness.

This is another activity that needs creativity. The worship outlines in this book all include creative intercessory activities that connect to the readings and themes of the day. If prayers are to be inclusive in all-age worship then it will be important to prepare well, thinking carefully about who leads and prepares, as well as the content. Silence for thought is also vital, which may be done as part of movement around the building, or as a moment of solitude within the gathering. Inviting people to write prayers is not always the best option. There are many in our churches who find the idea of writing something quickly and briefly an overwhelming challenge, and then there are those who have either lost or not yet developed the motor skills needed. It is very hard to distil onto a small Post-it note all the feelings of a heart full of anxiety over a daughter's marriage problems, or a mind full of images of death and suffering from the national news, or an imagination wondering whether Granddad will be well enough to play later that day. Invariably people end up writing one or two words such as 'love' or 'peace' in an attempt to capture all they are thinking.

Sadly a certain well-known high-street store no longer sells the scented, fabric, rose petals I have used for years in prayer activities. Each person, of every age, is invited to hold a petal and then drop it into the font as a sign of all their prayers that day. The leader then gathers the prayers together when everyone has returned to their seat. This allows everyone to make a response appropriate to their concerns. There are many other ideas for creative intercession, and more can be found in the liturgies and in the chapter on being multi-sensory in worship.

There are other activities that form part of the response. In many churches there will be a creed or statement of faith. Using the same form most of the time for an all-age service is important, and helps to build the sense of belonging. (Then, when there is an appropriate variation for a special festival, it stands out for everyone.) It also helps to create continuity with other forms of church service, so that a child or young person will feel at home in different churches. This is also true of the Lord's Prayer – as my niece discovered. It is helpful too if the form used, whether traditional or contemporary, is the same as that used in the local school.

✔ *Tip*

Sharing the peace

This is a valuable part of worship, helping to build community and introducing movement and energy into the worship. There are many different options to introduce the peace, and a short favourite from the Community of St Hilda is this:

**God makes peace within us – let us claim it.
God makes peace between us – let us share it.**[1]

This is straightforward and easy to understand and might be introduced by children and accompanied by actions, before the formal words and response are said. As with the opening responses, this is a very easy response to learn by heart:

Minister The peace of the Lord be always with you.

All **And also with you.**[2]

Celebrating

I have called this a subset of responding, but of course a eucharistic liturgy is a celebration from start to end. However, in the way in which liturgy unfolds, preparing the table, bringing gifts, and the eucharistic prayer flow naturally as a response to the hearing of God's word and the sense of relationship which has been built during the worship. There are many issues around all-age Eucharists and many debates about language and practice. Approximately 15 per cent of Anglican churches now admit children to Holy Communion before Confirmation, and in many other traditions bread and wine are readily shared with the whole gathered faith community. Perhaps more than anything it is important to remember that the Eucharist is a drama, and that the movement and actions will speak loudly if done with an intention to include.

➡ WE GO OUT

Many of us involved in planning and leading worship are so pleased to have offered creative and engaging ideas for a talk, for prayers, for music, that we breathe a sigh of relief and forget about endings. But good liturgy has a shape, and good inclusive all-age practices also have a shape. Programmes such as *Strictly Come Dancing* not only have a familiar beginning; they also have an equally familiar ending.

Even when the timing on live shows is clearly running late, they never forget to slip in that final invitation to 'keep dancing'. This is because these phrases act as markers or signposts, helping people to know that things are now moving to a different phase. In worship it is also the moment when we turn our attention from God to the world where we will bear witness to the good news in our daily lives at home, work or school.

✔ *Tip*

It is helpful if the ending is clear and strong, with simple words and actions that are recognizable.

Sometimes the notices will be included at this point, which can be very appropriate as news is shared and announced of the life of church going beyond Sunday. However notices can also be very long, full of insider jokes and references and have the potential to be exclusive. Keep them clear and engaging.

There will be a blessing, a last hymn and some final words. As with the opening hymn or song, it is good to end with a robust, familiar tune that signals a sense of moving on and engaging with the world.

✔ *Tip*

Where recessionals (a formal procession at the end of a service) are part of the tradition, there is a great opportunity to gather children into the movement outwards, reflecting the link between worship and mission, or to ensure that they are aware of what is happening.

In one church the children all stand on seats and wave as the minister and those who took part go by – a great mixture of formal liturgy and informal relationships! It is also important to reflect on what messages are being communicated by actions. If children are invited to come out front for a special blessing, this might be a way of recognizing that their lives are demanding and challenging, or it could be a way of indicating that the service is not really for everyone after all, but was 'something cosy for the little ones'. It may be appropriate to single out other groups from time to time, rather than just children.

On some worship occasions it may be appropriate to be giving away something at the end of the service. The obvious occasions when this happens are Palm Sunday and Mothering Sunday, but many churches also offer sweets at Christmas and eggs at Easter. These are not the only times to offer something; for example, the worship outline for February suggests handing out love-heart sweets to people as they leave, reminding them of the love they know and the love they need to share.

Finally, there may be refreshments on offer. This is often the time when all the good intentions of welcome and inclusion are forgotten as we catch up with friends or pass on messages and arrange diary dates. But including everyone in the worship gathering begins at the door and ends when they leave the building (although of course it is also far more than just the couple of hours spent in Sunday or mid-week worship). When interviewing children from small rural parishes we discovered that for many of them the experience of being the only children in the church was far from negative. In a church that is modelled around family and truly welcomes all ages, the one or two children present feel loved and valued. Adults talk to them, know about the rhythm of their lives as much as they know about adult concerns and implicitly make them feel included.

Skeletons and shapes: putting it together

Knowing that there is a clear structure to all-age worship comes as a great relief to many. It is not necessary to keep inventing a format for each service, but instead a strong framework or skeleton is a liberation. It holds things together. Different people can be invited to lead or prepare different sections within the overall structure. Music serves to hold the structure together and allow the worship to flow. But more than that, structure is a positive advantage in developing worship that works for whoever is present. It builds confidence and community, allows participation and engagement, all of which make it easier to create a real worshipping church which allows everyone from infant to elder to encounter and experience God. Liturgy really is a gift to all-age worship!

To think about

- In what ways is there an identifiable structure to the worship in your church? Is it different for different kinds of occasions?

- How important is it to include times of silence and stillness in worship for all ages together?

- How do you choose music to sing or to listen to for all-age worship?

Notes

1 *New Women Included*, London: SPCK, 1996, p. 55.
2 *New Patterns for Worship*, London: Church House Publishing, 2008, p. 65, A11.

2

Bodies, places and spaces

Churches are amazing spaces. Whether a whitewashed medieval stone building or a 1990s brick-built hall, these spaces are often the largest that we engage with during our week. If we go regularly to some of the larger parish churches or cathedrals found across the UK, we are probably entering one of the biggest spaces we will enter in our lives. Day after day I am privileged to watch and listen to regulars and visitors who engage with the wonder of a great cathedral. Each year we have hundreds of Year 6 children attending school leavers' services, and for many of the children, simply entering the space, seeing the immense size of the pillars, the huge expanses of stained glass, is a moment of wonder.

Recently I was visiting a straightforward Anglican church with modest numbers present for a normal parish Eucharist. There were some children visiting that day, and during the service they were playing in a special area set aside close to the front. Afterwards I decided to ask the mother and the children about their experience of church. This family were not church regulars at all – in fact, this was their third visit in connection with weddings and banns. Mum expressed the view that the younger child might like more toys to play with. My heart sank – surely church is about more than toys! Then I spoke to the 5-year-old directly. 'What do you like best about this church?' I asked. Without a moment's hesitation he stretched his arm up above his head to indicate the huge stained-glass window. 'I like this,' he said, and then swept his arm across the whole of the chancel area. 'And all of this.'

Space is really important. Children spend most of their lives split between two main spaces: home and school. Contemporary housing needs, coupled with changing expectations, mean that in recent years

homes have become more individual but also smaller. There are rows of modern detached houses, but the living space may be smaller than that found in a Victorian terrace. This may mean families live in homes with relatively limited communal space. Open-plan dining/kitchen/living areas can mean there is little opportunity to leave things around or to stretch out with a really big activity. Some homes don't have dining tables or areas where shared activities take place. Outside space can be at a premium, and many families feel unable to let children play in communal areas.

> **Space is really important**

School can be a great space. Colour, light, movement are everywhere. Buildings are designed to encourage learning but also to facilitate play and activity. The days when windows were high so that children would not be distracted by outside are long gone, as are the days when desks were in a fixed position, so all the children could sit still and see the 'blackboard' or the teacher on a raised dais at the front. Instead, classrooms are flexible spaces, with desks arranged in groups, with special areas for together times, display boards and resources. The children are not only able to look outside, but, particularly for younger children, there is a positive flow between inside and outside spaces. Learning is enhanced by the environment itself.

There are other public spaces that families visit. A great deal of thought goes into how the environment will support the primary activity that is taking place. Architecture and design work together to make shopping, sport, play, theatre a more positive experience. Over many centuries church architecture has employed the same principles. The shape of our buildings, the items that have been selected to be there, the colours and shapes have all been chosen for their symbolic value. Above all, the building is there to give glory to God, and to help those who gather to worship the One who is beauty and truth.

> The building is there to give glory to God, and to help those who gather worship the One who is beauty and truth

But when we gather for worship in these spaces, all that space, all that beauty, is put to one side. Routinely, worship takes place in the lower third of the building, with everyone facing forward in a manner reminiscent of the old-style schoolroom. Of course, in many of our churches, this is forced upon us by the presence of pews. Pews make straight lines, ensuring that everyone sits in their place and keeps their attention focused on the minister – and God. The strange thing is that even where churches have swapped pews for chairs, the chairs are frequently arranged in straight rows, facing the front. They often interlock, making any kind of flexibility almost impossible. So although our buildings are full of rich treasures, it can be very challenging trying to introduce movement into the space – challenging, but not impossible!

Using movement

I recently had the opportunity to lead worship at an annual family event in a very formal setting. It was a very daunting experience, combining formality, intellect (even the 2-year-olds are clever in a congregation largely made up of barristers and judges!), and a very beautiful and highly respected, yet restrictive, space. The restriction on movement was particularly acute because the pews are of the very traditional box type, with high dividers and locking doors. The only time I could be seen by everyone was when they were standing or I was in the pulpit.

However, there are ways of overcoming such restrictions on movement. In the prayers, I invited everyone to make clockwise quarter-turns – facing North, West, South, East. At each turn a simple meditation allowed people of all ages to travel in their minds to those they know across the world as well as to engage with world situations. The intercession ended with everyone becoming aware of themselves by placing a hand over the heart and focusing on God's presence. Children and adults alike both enjoyed and engaged with this prayer activity. Without disturbing the formality, without challenging the presence of pews, movement was introduced into the space.

There are many other ways of using movement to engage with the space. It is very simple to either look at or look away from key symbols in the church. For example, invite everyone to turn towards the back of the worship space, then someone opens the prayer by referring to the way we have literally turned our back on the things of God. Invite people to be still for a moment, before praying words of repentance. Then turn forward for the absolution, an assurance that God never turns his back on us. This is a very simple, graphic way of engaging people.

Other aspects of the building can be used in similar ways – turning to the font, the images in a particular window, or the door, etc. Using height and depth is also important. Inviting people to look up to the roof, to think about the grandeur of God and the immensity of his purposes for our lives is very effective. Invite people to feel the earth beneath their feet – even inviting those who are able, to lie down. Remind them of God's faithfulness in the place, referring to the history of the church and the community. Touching walls, looking beyond windows into the community around about, looking at memorial tablets are all ways of engaging mind and body in intercession.

All the suggestions so far have involved moving within a defined space, and are particularly suitable for small churches with limited opportunity for movement. However, it is sometimes appropriate for people to move about within the space. Introducing freer movement requires some careful thought and planning.

> ### ✔ Tip
>
> *Think through how people are going to begin the activity and end the activity: there will usually need to be some kind of explanation which needs to be given with confidence and an expectation that people are going to join in. This also needs to include an option for those with limited movement. Below is an example of how this might work.*

✔ **Tip**

Building a cairn prayer activity

Instructions

Explain the activity using these or similar words:

> In a moment, I am going to invite you all to come forward, collect a stone from one of the baskets the young people are holding, then walk to the front of the worship space and place your stone so that a cairn is built up. When you have placed your stone, please walk back to your seat down the side aisles. As you are moving, music will be playing. When everyone has returned to their seat, X will lead us in a prayer that gathers up all our thoughts.

Make sure you have people ready to hold the baskets/ containers with the stones.

Place someone at the front to monitor the cairn-building. This helps to create a sense that it is important and also creates confidence. Those of us who tend to worry about whether things are working can relax and stop worrying whether the stones are being put down in the right place!

Prime someone to start moving – but not a clergy person or other official or a child. This gives a message that the activity is for everyone. It is important that clergy join in with the movement, but simply in the flow of things.

Choose music with care – this depends on the focus of the activity. If it is reflective, then choose quieter music but with a strong rhythm – Celtic or folk tunes are often good. If the stone (or similar item) is being used as a symbol of praise or thanks, something livelier will be more suitable.

Gathering prayer – should be simple, pick up the themes of the activity and allow silence for reflection as well. For example, 'Lord God, hear our prayers today for the difficult situations in our world and for those whom we know are facing difficult times. Amen.'

Prayer stations

Other types of movement are also possible in some spaces, for example, creating prayer stations and inviting people to make their way to the locations to do something. Again, clarity of purpose and instructions are very important. Think about whether people are to move between all the different stations, or to choose one or two places to spend more time at, and make this clear. Decide if each station needs a facilitator to help people engage with the activity. Choose music that is suitable for the activity.

✔ **Tip**

It is not always appropriate or possible for the congregation to move around the space, but it is almost always possible for those taking part to move around.

Dramatic readings

Voices that come from different, particularly unexpected, places in the church can be very effective. In one church we did a dramatic reading of the temptations (see Luke 4.1–13), which began with someone striding across the chancel. Then suddenly, a man jumped onto one of the window sills and read the second temptation, before the final voice began to speak from the balcony. One of the advantages of doing the unexpected is that everyone present shares the same experience of surprise. It is not about singling one group out to give them an unusual moment, but rather that we are all equal at that moment.

✔ **Tip**

It is important with this kind of reading to think about how those who have hearing difficulties will take part, particularly if they are used to a hearing loop. It may be that giving out copies of the reading to those who need it is helpful, or it may be that an explanation is sufficient.

It is also important to rehearse any kind of reading that is out of the ordinary. This ensures that timing and impact are purposeful, not accidental.

Using processions

In an all-age Eucharist, much more can be made of a Gospel procession, which is already an opportunity to introduce movement. In some traditions, the Gospel is read from a central point in the church, and the Gospel book or Bible is carried to that place with appropriate ceremony, including responses and music. This signals to everyone that the core of our faith, the story of Jesus' life and teaching, is being proclaimed. Colour and drama can be added with music, banners, even incense where appropriate.

Using our bodies

The experience of worship is about the physicality of the worship space, but is also about the physicality of human beings. For just as the space has been designed and planned by human beings to help us give glory to God, so too our bodies themselves can be used in worship far more extensively than is usual. Worship needs to be multi-sensory as well as physical.

> The experience of worship is about the physicality of the worship space, but is also about the physicality of human beings

Most worship not only happens in a limited area of the available space, but it also only engages a limited part of the human body, and only one or two of the five senses with which we have been created. I might add a sixth sense here – not in any kind of mystical, intuitive way, but in the sense of our imaginations which can enable us to experience all kinds of situations and possibilities. When worship limits both movement and sensory activity there are a number of consequences for children and for adults.

Younger children, particularly preschool age groups, develop their knowledge and skills through experience. Toddlers discover the concepts of high and low, rough and smooth, warm and cool, not through physics lessons or books, but by moving about their space and touching, smelling, tasting the things they encounter. Anyone who takes an 18-month-old for a walk knows that it can take half an hour to get from the door to the gate as every single bit of ground becomes a moment of discovery. Gravel needs to run through fingers, earth needs to be tasted, feathers run over skin, flowers are sniffed at and a blade of grass held up in wonder. It's strange then that when it comes to worship, toddlers are given so few opportunities to handle creation and wonder at the Creator.

By the time children are 7 years old, their capacity for engaging with activities is enhanced by movement. It's a very irritating fact that children between 7 and 11 are able to multitask very effectively. It is easily possible to be listening to the teacher and simultaneously plaiting each other's hair. In fact it is not just possible, it is desirable for children of this age to use mind and body simultaneously. Any experience becomes more memorable for children when they are participants. not just observers. Educationalists know this, classrooms reflect this, and teachers use it effectively. Church is a much more positive experience for children if they use their bodies and their senses.

A friend of mine was leaving a typical Sunday service with her 7-year-old son. As he skipped along the path with her, he declared, 'I enjoyed that from the tip of my toes right up to heaven and back down again.' Two things had happened in the service that were different: first, he was invited to take the collection; second, the intercessions were based on the North, West, South, East ideas outlined earlier. Both these meant he was able to move legitimately (without anyone accusing him of wriggling and telling him to sit still) and both enabled him to take part fully and be responsible.

Engaging with different learning styles

The interesting thing is that many adults will also find multi-sensory movement more engaging than simply listening to words or looking at pictures. While it is true that some of us are verbal and auditory learners, there are also people who are kinaesthetic or visual learners. This means that doing something is always going to be more helpful than hearing about it.

✔ Tip

If we are creating worship for everyone present, it is also important to remember the needs of those with limited sensory abilities and movement. This can be where the use of the imagination is important. For example, in a confession activity which uses the parts of the body to focus thoughts, some people find it helpful to make the movements, while others find it sufficient to follow mentally.

Placing your hands over your eyes can be done literally, allowing children and others to move bodies and experience the sense of darkness. Others can simply follow in their imagination – which doesn't mean that the theme has been unhelpful.

Using our eyes

Using the sense of 'seeing' is perhaps the obvious place to start, as much of what is happening in our churches is about looking. We have already considered ways of moving and engaging with the visible aspects of our buildings in fresh ways, but there are also other ways of making sure that 'seeing' is purposefully used in worship. At a very basic level, it is important that what is there to look at it is well-presented and lovely.

✔ Tip

Involving children and young people in preparing the worship space is a way of helping them to engage with what is to happen and giving them real responsibility. This might be immediate, such as helping to set the table or arrange a visual display for worship, or more long term like working on a banner or vestments. This is a great opportunity for older people to work alongside children, sharing skills together and listening to each other's life experiences.

Two of the most valuable spiritual concepts are linked to seeing: the notion of reflecting and the idea of revelation. Both of these can be built into worship in creative ways that engage all ages. Using mirrors and other reflective surfaces can allow people to look at things differently. For example, a Christmas confession uses silver-surfaced baubles in which our reflection is distorted to encourage people to think about how we have distorted God's image in our own lives.

✔ Tip

Shiny surfaces are particularly attractive to younger children, so placing mirror objects into a children's area is helpful.

Revelation is that moment when we move from not seeing to seeing, both literally and metaphorically. It can be a slow process or a dramatic moment. This is when the use of light and darkness is so effective in creating an atmosphere in which everyone can engage in worship. The sudden appearance of candlelight in the distance, echoing the starlight of Christmas or the dawn of Easter day, is a moment that draws attention. Likewise hiding something until a special moment in the worship can have a great impact. One of my most useful objects is a mirror concealed in a silver frame behind closing doors: looking for one moment at one's own reflection is challenging but thought-provoking.

Technology vs. home-made

Many churches have increased the range of things available to look at by introducing technology, with images used to enhance hymns, prayers and talks. Sometimes this is very helpful, but for children it can also be a very passive activity, with echoes of the very thing society worries about for their well-being. I once did the same talk in two churches. It was a talk that required images of famous people. In one church we projected them onto a screen so everyone could see. In a much smaller country church, the technology was unavailable, so instead I printed out the images on A4 sheets, laminated them and attached them to sticks. I then invited people (not just children) to volunteer to parade them around the church showing them as I talked. It added a whole new dimension of engagement as people turned in their seats and the families walked about. Several of the children who carried pictures asked to keep them. As one father said to me after the service: 'Thanks to you I now have a two-year-old who can't be separated from a picture of George Bush!!'

Using touch

There are a surprising number of opportunities in worship to use our sense of touch. There are textures and surfaces all around us – and consciously touching as part of worship can help people to engage. For example, deliberately placing hands onto the wood of the pew, feeling the history, engaging with memories, can all serve as an introduction to a prayer activity.

✔ Tip

Sometimes it is appropriate to give people an object to hold at a key point in the worship – seeds, stones, feathers, acorns, sweets, all these and many more have been used as a focus.

It could be that people are invited to move forward and touch something – in some traditions there is a practice of touching the cross on Good Friday, but this could be extended – for example, moving forward and touching the water in the font as a sign of renewed commitment.

There is also making contact with other human beings, which happens routinely in the peace. This moment of exchanged human contact is very important, reminding us that we are called to be a body together. It is very egalitarian and a great moment for everyone present to be involved.

I encourage the sharing of the peace in all services, not just at the Eucharist. Sometimes it is appropriate to hold hands and make human contact at another point in the worship. A word of warning though – some people, including children, find it very uncomfortable to be asked to hold hands. In fact, this is one of those moments that can lead to giggling and squirming – and that's just some of the adults! A good substitute is to invite palm-to-palm contact, which is less intimate and feels like a gesture of support and solidarity.

There are also activities that invite people to touch or hold parts of their own bodies. Simple prayer actions like using each finger for a different focus are relatively easy to do, and even those who are very self-conscious can engage unobtrusively. Changing posture can have a similar effect, with the added advantage of adding movement for those who find sitting still challenging. For example, standing tall, sitting, kneeling, and placing head in hands are all postures which are acceptable for prayer, but using them consciously helps people of all ages engage with what is happening, perhaps discovering something in a fresh way.

Using taste

Being multi-sensory starts to get more difficult at this point! Yet when given the task of brainstorming activities using all the senses, worship leaders can usually come up with one or two ideas. Taste is not an unfamiliar idea in Scripture! Thankfully, God uses images of banqueting and wine-tasting to describe the coming kingdom, and not just a few leftovers either. God is a generous God, a God of feasting as well as fasting, who uses images of abundance to affirm his blessing and his presence. Hospitality is also a key to the spread of the kingdom of God, one of the core characteristics of God's people. So tasting foods sounds like a good part of worship! It is intrinsic to the Eucharist, as we share bread and wine together.

✔ Tip

There are other opportunities for including taste within a worship service. For example, at the beginning of a celebration of God's abundance, as the congregation gathered, people walked about carrying platters piled high with garlic dough balls, offering them to everyone. As the beginning of the service, a trumpet sounded. Then a voice called, 'Come, buy bread without price!' (cf. Isaiah 55.1) and the cry was taken up and echoed by other voices in the room. That set the theme for the whole celebration.

On another occasion we gave everyone two squares of chocolate as they arrived, telling them to eat the chocolate and save the foil. Later the foil was used in the prayers as part of Fairtrade fortnight.

Tasting things often injects a sense of fun, good humour and the unexpected into worship. Humour is one of the key elements that makes Pixar films so good for all ages. It works in different ways at different levels and can be a great equalizer as well. The moment when someone tastes something unexpectedly good (or horrid!) is often a source of laughter (although care needs to be taken never to laugh at someone). And taste needs to spill over into the after worship moments, with good food available, even something to reflect on the theme of the service. After a sermon on the bread of life, we all had lots of lovely home-made bread during coffee-time!

Using our sense of smell

Home-made bread brings us to the idea of using smell in worship, perhaps the trickiest of all the senses, although like taste it is very much part of biblical worship. If we could travel through the Bible in a way akin to the Jorvik experience at York, our noses would be assaulted by the smell of worship. There would, of course, be the smell of sacrifice, but perhaps also the smell of incense, the smell of perfume, and the smell of creation itself as much worship would take place outdoors.

For many churches moving some or all of the liturgy outdoors could itself be part of a worship service. For example, in a small rural church on a beautiful June day, we decided to take the prayers outside. It was an inspired moment, as everyone trooped out of the building and engaged in the multi-sensory experience that is God's wonderful world. People took off sandals to feel the grass, let the sun warm their skin, smelt the lilacs wafting on the breeze, listened to the birdsong – it was just a shame we had no early strawberries to eat as well!

More traditionally, incense has been part of many major festivals, although this is clearly not for all churches. It can be done in more subtle ways than a full-blown thurifer and thurible. Scented candles are common in many homes, and introducing

them into worship can add a subtle reminder of how our prayers can rise before God. In another setting, incense grains were placed in bowls and two people walked around, wafting the incense over the worshippers. On another occasion, we simply sprayed perfume into the air during a prayer time to remind us of God's presence with us, and I've already mentioned the scented rose petals briefly.

✔ Tip

To make scented rose petals: buy some low-price artificial roses, and then (perhaps when you are feeling stressed!), pull them apart. Place the petals into a bowl of water containing an essential oil. Soak for about two hours, then leave to dry.

Place the petals into a lovely bowl, and invite people to come forward to pick up a petal, then move to the font and drop it in, praying for whatever is in mind, or perhaps focusing on childhood. Petals are also shaped like tears, which brings another dimension to the activity. The perfume rises like incense before God, prayer continuing even when the congregation has left.

Using our ears

Listening is clearly the sense that is at the centre of our worship, where words tend to dominate, whether said, sung or read. The problem with words is that for many people it is not easy to access them quickly or with facility. This might be because reading is not yet a skill someone has mastered, or because sight is fading, or simply because words are not the medium with which someone is at ease. However, words delivered well can have great power. This might be as simple as using different voices in different ways, or as basic as making sure the readers read well. Reading aloud is a gift which can be developed. There are 9-year-olds who are brilliant at reading aloud, and 39-year-olds who are so embarrassed it would be better if they hadn't felt obliged. Rehearsal and practice helps, as well as experimenting with different versions.

Bible versions for all-age worship

There are some good Bible adaptations for children, such as the Big Bible Story Book or the Lion Storyteller Bible. These can be helpful, but it is also important for children and adults to know that the things being read are from the Bible. The Contemporary English Version is a straightforward translation, particularly good for reading aloud, and the NRSV is also very clear, especially if read well.

The important thing is to check beforehand. If using a dramatic version of the text, make sure that it helps to make the story more engaging as, done without preparation, dramatic readings can be very difficult to follow.

There are many creative ways of delivering the word of God. Some are familiar like drama, others less so, like choral reading or poems that either elucidate or complement the text. As with other spoken sections of the service, delivering words from different locations and from unexpected places also makes a big impact.

There is also music – participating in singing and music-making as well as listening to music performed by others is important in bringing people closer to an encounter with God. Many children and young people are no longer familiar with singing; music is something to listen to and watch being performed, and it may be helpful to include some recorded music during a service. This might include secular as well as sacred music, especially where a song is popular and has lyrics that resonate with everyday experiences.

There are also a whole range of other sounds that can be used, including bells, both large and small, musical instruments and various sound effects.

Illustrating the story of the storm on the lake with some dramatic noises can be very engaging, as might be the loud clattering of pots and pans to mark the resurrection on Easter Day!

The absence of sound is also an important part of worship, but many people are afraid of using silence in all-age services. There is a fear that children cannot cope with silence and need to move from one loud noise to another. In reality, many children long for times of stillness and quiet. The key is to help them get to that place, and give them clear direction.

Make sure silence is always intentional in worship rather than accidental, and used to dramatic or symbolic effect. Together with darkness, silence is a powerful aid to worship, especially in seasons of waiting or at times of sadness.

Using our imagination

Human beings are amazing and the human mind especially so. Without moving from a cold, gloomy church we can travel in our imaginations to places of warmth and splendour. We can recreate exotic animals, high mountains, roaring rivers and almost any kind of experience, as long as we have a hook to start with. Getting everyone to close their eyes and travel on an imaginary journey, perhaps back to Galilee or to some amazing part of God's creation, is something that everyone who is present can engage with. It's the ultimate multi-sensory experience, and we should not be afraid to draw on it in the liturgy and in the teaching that we offer.

Using bodies, place and space

All-age experiences are far from two-dimensional. Families who are engaged at a theme park or a rugby match are listening, seeing, touching, smelling and tasting all that is on offer, making the whole event memorable in body as well as mind. Developmentally, children have been created to discover the world through senses and movement. Unlike adults they cannot hide their feelings behind a composed mask – they need to express their enthusiasm or disdain in action and energy. This means that worship for everyone present needs to make full use of the whole gamut of human creativity to ensure that we are able to engage emotionally, intellectually and physically as we encounter God and offer him praise that brings glory to his name and unites the body of Christ.

To think about

- How could you make more effective use of the worship space you have available? What features are there and what story do they tell or emotions do they evoke?

- Which of the senses do you find helpful in worship, and which the most difficult to include?

- Why do you think that multi-sensory and physical activities help children and adults to enter into worship together?

3

Mystery and wonder

It may seem strange to include mystery and wonder as key components of good all-age worship. Yet the sharing of moments of awe and astonishment is one of the things that help cross-generational groups to build shared memories. When a parent and child are together at a rugby or soccer game and recognize a moment of immense skill, or when they see a victory emerge from what was a sure defeat, a sense of having been present together and witnessing something extraordinary is very important.

In a different cross-generational context, I took my 23-year-old nephew to see *The Woman in Black*[1] (a play adapted from the novel by Susan Hill) at a West End theatre. We are still talking about how the intense atmosphere of mystery and suspense was created. And only recently I entered into a conversation about this play with a group of teenagers who had been to see it – the same themes, the same fascination emerged. Everyone is captivated by mystery.

One of the very earliest games that children enjoy is the game 'peek-a-boo'. As soon as a baby is able to recognize that a person who disappears can reappear, this game can be an endless source of delight for both infant and adult. For the baby, there is the constant astonishment that the missing person – or object – reappears. For the older person, child, parent, grandparent, there is the delight of creating

> Psychologists and theologians believe that there is something intrinsic to human identity about this game, with its themes of presence and absence, mystery and revelation

that astonishment. Psychologists and theologians believe that there is something intrinsic to human identity about this game, with its themes of presence and absence, mystery and revelation. This instinct is then picked up in games, activities and stories.

Popular and successful stories for very young children often pick up on this sense of quest. The children's book, *Peepo*, by Janet Ahlberg and Allan Ahlberg,[2] is a retelling of the game, and many other pre-reading books involve objects that are hidden and have to be discovered.

> **We all like astonishing tales because they touch the nerve of the ancient instinct of astonishment. This is proved by the fact that when we are very young children we do not need fairy tales: we only need tales. A child of seven is excited by being told that Tommy opened a door and saw a dragon. A child of three is excited by being told that Tommy opened a door.**[3]

Although G. K. Chesterton was writing over a century ago, this reflection is still true, even in a world of computers and virtual realities. In fact, many of the games and programmes children engage with on screen pick up on the same themes of astonishment. This sense of wonder is something that is also utilized in the best kind of theme parks, discovery centres and museums. Adults, teenagers and young children are all astonished as the mysteries of the world we live in, past or present, are unpacked using contemporary technology to create moments of wonder. Even in something as entertainment-focused as Disneyland there is a shared astonishment as the characters previously seen as two-dimensional come to life.

Wonder in worship

However, astonishment and amazement can also be translated into a series of entertaining tricks and illusions. They can appear in the 'children's talk' as a kind of special effect, rather than being an integral part of worship. In worship, there also needs to be a sense of awe and wonder, so that worship itself expresses something of this amazement, both at the idea of God and also at the good news that God should chose to become known to humankind. This is the most astonishing and amazing discovery of all. To fully engage with this we need worship that is transcendent as well as accessible.

In the last chapter we looked at ways in which multi-sensory activities and the creative use of space can begin to ensure that the experience of worship offers an opportunity for all ages to be awed and amazed. In a culture that is often focused on the functional and the technological, beauty can be overlooked. In a world obsessed with celebrity and status, beauty can be misunderstood as only concerned with cosmetic appearance. In worship, beauty is there to enable everyone to share in an encounter with God. It is not about monetary value, nor even aesthetic excellence (though that will play a part). Rather it is about opportunities through worship for people to become aware of something that is beyond the ordinary, yet tangible within the everyday.

> **Worship is about opportunities through worship for people to become aware of something that is beyond the ordinary, yet tangible within the everyday**

Limitations of the educational model of children's work

Work with children in and through church has its roots in a strongly educational model, focusing less on an experience of awe, and more on developing understanding. The first Sunday school, founded by Robert Raikes in 1762, grew out of his desire to offer children a way out of poverty, and an opportunity to become good citizens. Classes were focused on reading and writing, listening to religious and moral stories and memorizing biblical texts. Sunday schools were places where learning and understanding would develop, and children would acquire practical skills and a moral framework that would help ensure that they had the chance of fulfilling their potential. They were not really about worship, in the sense of an encounter with the awe and wonder of the transcendent God.

This educational approach to faith has shaped much of our work with children, and also many of our worries as well. Adults are concerned about how much children know, or whether they have learned the right stories, and less concerned about how much they have experienced the presence of God. In recent years psychologists have discovered that children are inherently capable of engaging with mystery and of living with paradox (see Recommended reading, p. 101).

Seeing the world from a child's perspective

Children live all the time with partial understanding of the world. It's the nature of childhood. There have been some films and documentaries that try to help us see the world again from the perspectives of childhood, where we meet people at knee level, not eye level and where we are constantly only seeing partially in any situation. I have often wondered how strange the world must seem viewed from the bottom tier of one of those double-decker pushchairs! Children's experience of the world is like those puzzles which show everyday objects from strange angles and the challenge is to guess what it is. It is something that was captured in Rolf Harris's marvellous catchphrase, 'Can you see what it is yet?' Children are used to not having the full picture – it is the developmental journey they are on, and awe, mystery, astonishment and wonder are daily experiences as more of the picture comes into view.

In reality, it is not either/or but rather both/and . . . there are wonderful stories and truths that we need to share with children. But it is not the head knowledge that gives them a life-long passion for the things of God: it is the shared experience of something other, an encounter with God in worship. Sadly, a preoccupation with understanding and education has meant that we become overly concerned with 'making sure the children

> The challenge is to use enough words to make sense, without losing music, poetry and mystery, and allowing symbols to remain symbols, with their deep sense of the sacred

understand'. The challenge is to use enough words to make sense, without losing music, poetry and mystery, and allowing symbols to remain symbols, with their deep sense of the sacred.

When I invite adults to talk about their earliest memories of God, sometimes they will talk about moments of solitude, often in places that were beautiful to them at that time. When asked to choose images that reflect those recollections, they pick scenery, or images of children alone in a wide space. Some choose photos or drawings of churches. Many adults will talk about being in church and letting the words of Evensong wash over them, and sensing something valuable, experiencing a sense of encounter with otherness that is beyond articulating. I was a church-deprived child. But I found a copy of the Book of Common Prayer, probably a christening present, and I used to sit in bed reading hymns and prayers! My favourite lines were these:

> Immortal, invisible, God only wise
> In light inaccessible hid from our eyes . . .

I hadn't a clue what those words meant, but they moved something deep in my inner being, even as an 8-year-old reading by the fading light of a summer evening.

More recently I did some work with children talking about forgiveness. One 5-year-old, not from a church family or a church school, talked with real intensity about the mystery of forgiveness, before sighing and saying, 'And sometimes it's too hard so I read my Bible to help me feel better.'[4] And into my head popped an image of a small girl sitting up in bed, taking her christening gift of a children's Bible off the shelf and alone, reading it, and touching the mystery.

Recent research by Kate Adams revealed that over a third of the children she interviewed had had dreams or experiences with a spiritual dimension, that they never talked about with adults.[5] This is largely because they do not think that adults will

acknowledge the experience and treat it with respect. Children are able to use the language of mystery.

Immensely popular films, books, TV shows, draw on archetypes of light and darkness, sacrifice and death, love and loss. And that's just an episode of *Doctor Who*!

Worship, and liturgy as the framework for worship, should enable children and adults to encounter the mystery of God, as well as giving them opportunities for exuberant praise and thanks. I have often been amazed at how engaged children will be with

Taizé or Celtic styles of worship, which are rich in symbolism, involve silence and repetitive singing, and a lot of candles. We should not be afraid of engaging children with the whole

> We should not be afraid of engaging children with the whole breadth of tradition, and having an expectation that they will respond

breadth of tradition, and having an expectation that they will respond. Worship is more about experience than comprehension.

'But isn't it boring for them?'

There is often a real difficulty for churches with a strong eucharistic tradition around all-age worship. Some churches decide to introduce 'family worship', perhaps monthly, as non-eucharistic, lively and short. Often this is because we are fearful that the Eucharist will be inaccessible and 'boring' and, perhaps above all, too long. Long is not a synonym for bad, and short is not a synonym for good: it is very

> Long is not a synonym for bad, and short is not a synonym for good: it is very possible for children to be bored in short worship and engaged in something long

possible for children to be bored in short worship and engaged in something long.

This was brought home in a very real way after we organized a quiet day for 8- to 11-year-olds. As the children arrived, including three boys in football kit bouncing a ball, a little voice whispered to me that this was not one of my better ideas! However, as the day unfolded, this group of very ordinary children reached a level of intense silence that astonished the retreat house staff – and us! We had once again underestimated the spiritual capacity of children. They engaged in two-hour-long periods of silence, were offered a range of activities, a programme and lots of direction. At the end, we asked them for some feedback. They were universally enthusiastic and the number one word used to describe the day was 'fun'.

This led me to do some more work with children to unpack just what the word 'fun' really means, and its opposite – 'boring'. Many adults assume the word 'fun' equates to silliness, mess, noise and entertainment, and indeed it can. However, what it really means is: 'I was engaged with that.' To be bored simply means, 'You have failed to engage me.' This has little to do with the length of time, and everything to do with what is going on. I remember taking two children, aged 7 and 10, to an outdoor performance of *A Midsummer Night's Dream*. The verdict: 'That was better than *Star Wars*!!' Each half was about 75 to 90 minutes in length, and their attention was absolute. Likewise the rugby match: 90 minutes in total, and no concessions to children!

Some families go to church with a passionate belief that this is something that matters, and yes, sometimes it will be less inspiring than others, but the starting point is an expectation that being there matters. If we begin with an anxiety about how long the service is, maybe we are already assuming that it doesn't have the potential to engage. However, we do need to be realistic about very young children, and make sure that there is the possibility of moving away or moving around without feeling embarrassed.

> We do need to be realistic about very young children, and make sure that there is the possibility of moving away or moving around without feeling embarrassed

The Eucharist for everyone

The challenge then is to create a 'fun' engaging act of worship – and there is nothing more engaging than the mystery of the Eucharist! As a sacrament, the Eucharist is a profound expression of the way in which God meets us in our human lives, drawing close to us and enabling us to draw close to one another. Children and adults from a wide range of ages and experiences use surprisingly similar words when asked to describe what Communion means to them. The themes that emerge can be grouped into three key areas: mystery, belonging and nurture. The mystery is partly because the Eucharist cannot be adequately explained, and partly in expressing something of a very real sense of the presence of God. Belonging is about feeling part of the body of Christ and sharing something with others who gather. Nurture covers those words that describe being given strength and encouragement for living or, as one 4-year-old expressed it, 'I feel like bigger inside.'

> Children and adults from a wide range of ages and experiences use surprisingly similar words when asked to describe what Communion means to them

There are many reasons for awe and astonishment in the Eucharist. There is the incredible reminder that God meets us in ordinary things, transforms the ordinary stuff of life into the mystery of eternity. Bread, everyday basic food stuff; wine, ordinary fare for special times: these become for us the food of heaven, and more. The words that we speak at this point are themselves astonishing. In every aspect of the liturgy, God is revealing Godself as One who trusts human endeavours as capable of becoming means of grace. The actions and words together should be moments that enable everyone present to articulate some form of 'wow'.

A second source of astonishment is the way in which a diverse group of people becomes one. As I wait, either to receive Communion or afterwards, sometimes I simply watch the people moving forward. I am often moved by this visible evidence that God's invitation is truly to all people, whatever their circumstances. No one needs to justify why they are there; no explanations are necessary. Simply by being at the table, we are being gathered and accepted. The whole action of the Eucharist is also an astonishingly simple pointer to Jesus. In just a few words and a few gestures the entire history of salvation pivoted around the death and resurrection of Jesus is there for us, time after time: so very straightforward and so very accessible.

And yet, it seems so difficult to enable it to be an occasion when everyone present touches the mystery and the wonder. For some the presence and participation of children in every way is now normal practice. Not only are children in the service, they also receive bread and wine. This is not the place to recap the arguments as to why this is good practice – there are many places to look for advice and discussion (see p. 101 for Recommended reading). But it is worth reminding ourselves that, whether children are receiving a blessing or bread and wine, they are equal with every other person present in their inability to comprehend this mystery, and their capacity for being astounded by the grace and presence of God.

✔ Tip

Involving children in the Eucharist

There are many practical ways of involving children, not just in taking part in the worship activities themselves but in the planning and delivery. Many churches involve children and families in taking the offering or bringing forward the bread and the wine. But it can go further. Traditionally, children often act as servers at the altar, handling sacred things and a visible reminder to the members of the congregation that they are part of the worship. Even where this is not the practice, involving children in setting the table is a great way of engaging them. This could be as simple as placing things onto the table or as comprehensive as starting with the altar cloth itself and adding all that is needed. They can then remain at the table as the prayer is offered. Some of the Common Worship *eucharistic prayers allow children to be active participants, notably Prayer D, when children can say the words, 'This is his story', inviting the congregational response, 'This is our song.' There are also some new eucharistic prayers, currently being finalized, which have been specifically written for services with significant numbers of children present. These will also include opportunities for children to participate in the prayer.*

Recently, I was guest preacher in a church at ease with children present around the Communion table. A small girl, about 6 years old, had adopted me as her new best friend, and glued herself to my side during the eucharistic prayer. When I moved forward to offer the bread, she simply stood next to me. No words passed between us. But out of the corner of my eye I became aware that something was happening. After a few minutes of observation, she had clearly decided that something needed to be done. It wasn't enough to let people receive the bread, then move in front of her to the chalice. I realized that she was bowing to each person after they had received the bread, not in any trivial or light-hearted way, but as a formal gesture to fit with the solemnity she had perceived. Some adults ignored her, but several bowed back! It was a wonderful liturgical moment, and I was reminded of Miriam who stepped out and led the women in the dance in Exodus 15. This is not to suggest that this is something to build into the liturgy, but rather a reminder of children's own capacity to respond, and even to initiate response to worship.

In a different church, with a more formal style of worship, toddlers and carers are invited to come and sit directly around and in front of the Communion table after the table has been set and until the distribution. During the singing of a hymn, several bean bags were scattered, and families moved forward, mums and dads holding little ones, and helping them engage with all that was happening. Older children sat on the front seats and along the centre aisle, allowing them to see what was happening and yet keeping them connected to the whole congregation. This kind of initiative helps to ensure that children are very much part of what is happening, rather than a sudden rush up to the Communion table just before the distribution ends. It is particularly important when children do receive bread and wine that they are present for most of the service, returning from any special teaching at the peace. If some people are not present, then the possibility of everyone meeting God in worship, word and sacrament is massively diminished. The absence of children is not just about removing their chance of an encounter with Jesus, but also limits the possibility for others to encounter mystery.

> The absence of children is not just about removing their chance of an encounter with Jesus, but also limits the possibility for others to encounter mystery

As Richard Giles expresses it:

> An assembly without children is a deficient, incomplete assembly, not only because children are a vital chunk of any cross-section of humanity, nor because they represent our future, but because they are identified in the Judaeo-Christian tradition as the bearers of the mystery.[6]

Engaging with mystery is experiential. Encounter is about the coming together of words, silence, music, symbol in a way that allows those moments of amazement at God's grace to happen. It's stating the obvious, yet still worth reminding ourselves, that the Eucharist is the whole act of worship, not just the prayer said at the Communion table. It is also worth remembering that the minister is acting as president for the worship of the whole people of God. Being present through the whole movement of the liturgy is an important part of growing into a sense of belonging, and is part of developing the kind of understanding that is not about theory but about practice. (If we think back to the rugby match, remember that the children stay for the whole game from their earliest visits.)

When putting together an all-age Eucharist much worry is centred around the eucharistic prayers themselves and whether they are accessible or comprehensible, but the prayer is only three to five minutes out of the whole experience. There is much that can be done throughout the worship to help ensure that whoever is present has the possibility of an encounter with God.

Although the eucharistic prayer itself may be relatively short, there is a great deal that happens around it which can be difficult to understand, and can take rather a long time without much opportunity for participation. Thought needs to be given as to which form of words are used after the Lord's Prayer.

✔ Tip

Not everything is mandatory, and even for those elements that are, there are alternative versions available which may well be more accessible to a wider range of people. For example, it is not essential to use the Agnus Dei nor the Prayer of Humble Access and there are some short forms of invitation available.

Other things might simply be about mechanics – how quickly the congregation begins moving forward or what happens if a large number of helpers need to receive Communion. Cathedrals and larger churches are often very good at the mechanics, and much can be learned by observing how it's done when Communion is distributed to two thousand people effectively. However, even with the best mechanisms in place there may be a hiatus during the distribution of between 5 and 15 minutes. To children this can seem like nothing is happening – indeed, many adults behave as if nothing is happening!

It may be appropriate to do something at this point. For example, on one occasion, each person was invited to pick up a large luggage label as they returned from receiving Communion, and then took a few minutes to create a prayer that reflected what they would be doing in the week ahead. These were then tied onto suitcases at the back of the church, and incorporated into the final dismissal. This is not about keeping children quiet so adults are not disturbed, but helping them to stay engaged with all that is happening so that the possibilities of encounter remain.

Throughout the Eucharist there are moments of mystery, moments when the grace of God is called into view. These are moments when silence and symbol can be used powerfully. Taking time to recognize the act of saying sorry and the confirmation of forgiveness is one such moment, but equally so might be the offering of prayers in confident belief that God is at work: astonishing! It may be that sometimes we need to make space to hear of how prayer is helping in individual and community lives – another moment of mystery.

> **Throughout the Eucharist there are moments of mystery, moments when the grace of God is called into view**

I once took a 12-year-old to a solemn Eucharist for Ash Wednesday in a great cathedral. We did everything: incense, burning of ash, ashing foreheads, singing the Gospel, plainsong, semi-darkness, silence. Afterwards I heard him on the phone to his parents. 'I've just been to this dead weird service, with dead weird music, where they did dead weird things and it was, just weird! It was awesome!'

Mystery is mysterious – as are human beings. We can observe good practice, identify the elements that make spaces for awe and wonder to break through, but in the end life is surprising, God is beyond anything we can imagine, and humans are unpredictable. Whether it's the shared family moment when a potentially tense situation spills into joyful laughter or the solemnly weird liturgy that lodges in a teenage mind, mystery and wonder are core components of the multi-generational experience.

To think about

- What things have you noticed children saying that show their capacity for astonishment and awe?
- What is your own earliest 'spiritual' memory – a sense of something other in the world – which may or may not be in a Christian framework?
- In what ways do you experience the Eucharist as an occasion of mystery and wonder?

Notes

1 *The Woman in Black* is a play adapted from the novel of the same name by Susan Hill, first published by Hamish Hamilton, 1983.
2 Janet Ahlberg and Allan Ahlberg, *Peepo*, Harmondsworth: Picture Puffin, 1983.
3 G. K. Chesterton, quoted in Jerome Berryman, *Children and the Theologians: Clearing the Way for Grace*, Harrisburg, Penn.: Morehouse Publishing, 2010.
4 Paraphrased from Anne Richards and Peter Privett, *Through the Eyes of a Child*, London: Church House Publishing, 2009, p. 158.
5 Kate Adams, *Unseen Worlds*, London: Jessica Kingsley, 2010.
6 Richard Giles, *At Heaven's Gate*, Norwich: Canterbury Press, 2010, p. 23.

4

Universal stories – it happens to us all

Creating worship that has the potential to engage everyone present needs structure and pattern, it needs to be multi-sensory, it needs to have moments of mystery, but perhaps above all else, it needs to connect with the lives of each person present. And the tool that allows this to happen is story. Story is one of those words, like myth, that has somewhat changed in its meaning. It's easy to think 'story' is something fabricated and lightweight, placing it into direct contrast with the serious business of bearing witness to the truth about God, God's people and God's world. But a story is simply a vehicle. A story is a construction that enables a sequence of events, actions, words and ideas to be held together in a way that makes it comprehensible to others. We all tell stories every single day. Over a coffee with friends, someone will say, 'Do you know what happened to me/my child/my neighbour this morning?' and so the 'story' will begin, an account of an event which has been edited and formed into a means of communication.

> It's easy to think 'story' is something fabricated and lightweight, placing it into direct contrast with the serious business of bearing witness to the truth about God, God's people and God's world

The power of story: learning from Pixar

It is the power of stories that is at the heart of all the successful all-age events in our culture, and no organization seems to have understood this better than Pixar animation. Films like *Toy Story*, *Finding Nemo*, *Up* and *Shrek* are not just for children. Yes, there is the immense skill and appeal of the high-quality animation and script, but even more important are the stories.

As Robert Velarde writes in *The Wisdom of Pixar*: 'Even though we may be watching toys or cars that are brought to life, or monsters or even rats, these characters contain a quality of reality to which we can relate.'[1] One of my favourite scenes in *Toy Story* comes shortly after Buzz Lightyear realizes that he is not really a space-ranger, he is actually a toy. This happens at a critical moment: Buzz and Woody are trapped in Sid's room, where he is intending to tie them to a rocket on the next day. Sid is a nasty piece of work! Woody needs Buzz to help him get free so they can plan to escape, but Buzz is sunk into despair. There follows an amazing dialogue as Woody tries to persuade Buzz that he is of immense value. There is tension and suspense. The scene fades as Buzz looks at the sole of his foot and sees the name of his owner, 'Andy', inscribed there. The next scene sees Buzz helping Woody to break free . . .

This is a great example of a universal theme. Whether aged 3, 33, 63, we all have moments when we have failed, and as adults we have times when we hit rock bottom, feeling that all that we thought we were has come to nothing. It's a crisis of identity, a crisis of self-worth.

Great all-age stories do not avoid darkness and pain, sadness and loss. There are moments of change and transition, exploring how we all cope with these moments: both *Toy Story 3* and *Up* are films which adults find particularly engaging as they explore the impact of ageing itself, yet they still appeal to children. It is not surprising that adults are the ones moved to tears.

> Great all-age stories do not avoid darkness and pain, sadness and loss

Learning from children's literature

The best children's books have the same quality. Whether a century-old classic like *Anne of Green Gables*[2] or a modern classic like *War Horse*,[3] issues of loss, death and grief are faced as part of life's experience.

Some commentators on children's literature detect a move in recent years towards a gritty realism in children's books. Jacqueline Wilson's stories deal with abandonment, personal moral dilemmas, living in care, coping with needy adults and many other topics. But these topics have always been there in books read by children and adults alike, whether *David Copperfield*[4] or *The Secret Garden*,[5] because they are part of life's experiences.

If we look at 'classic' stories that have stood the test of time, we will find the same kind of universal quality, whether the story is primarily aimed at children or adults. There are differences between a book or film that is simply for children and something that has a universal quality. One of those differences is whether the context of the book is more important than the theme. If it is, then those individuals, of whatever age, who enjoy the film or book are primarily interested in that context: we read because it's about space, not because it's about life issues. A context might be starting school, the universal theme is facing new beginnings. *The Silver Sword*[6] might be set in Poland in the Second World War, but it speaks of courage and friendship in a timeless way. Stories that cross boundaries manage to focus on the universal theme as well as the foreground issue which provided the initial attraction for the child or adult reader.

For example, the story of David and Goliath may be of great interest to a child because it concerns a child of the same age who is picked out to fight a giant against incredible odds. But it also carries a strong universal theme, familiar to us at various stages of life, of facing impossible tasks, carrying a responsibility that seems too big and finally overcoming the giants in our lives.

A story for very young children, *The Tiger Who Came to Tea*,[7] is a delightfully humorous story with great illustrations and is immensely appealing to small children, but it also resonates with adults as it explores themes of acceptance, difference and the unexpected. Many of us are familiar with the Narnia stories which also have this appeal across boundaries. Adults read these books, watch these films, and as Christians have little difficulty in identifying the Christian subtext. Recently I watched the film version of *The Lion, the Witch and the Wardrobe*[8] with a churchgoing child, who was amazed when I pointed out the parallels to the Jesus story. For her, the film had worked on the level of story, adventure and characters.

One of the greatest secrets about all-age communication is that it does not have to speak to everyone in the same way at the same time. What an adult sees, hears or reads in a book may be very different from how a child sees, hears or reads the same thing – but that does

> One of the greatest secrets about all-age communication is that it does not have to speak to everyone in the same way at the same time

not mean that one or other is wrong, or that the story has failed.

Liturgy as storytelling

The good news for those of us trying to bring great all-age communication into the life of the Church is that we have an abundance of stories, all of which are exploring these universal themes. The liturgy or act of worship is itself an act of storytelling. It is the story of God's people coming together and journeying on in the presence of God and then being trusted with the task of proclaiming the gospel and living out God's love in the world. In the Eucharist we are very specifically retelling the story of Jesus' life and death, calling it to mind directly, and indirectly mirroring the themes of God's grace freely offered. However, within the structure of a service, there will also be a specific point when we focus on the story of our faith and try to connect with our lives.

The talk for everyone

First, we usually offer a story or a text from Scripture and then we give a talk which should (but may not) relate to the story of the text. The talk is often one of the most challenging parts of an all-age service, and can be where the overall intent of engaging everyone present stands or falls. There are all kinds of pitfalls. Sometimes there is so little difference from an adult sermon that the children go off into the corner to do colouring even though the service is meant to include them. That tells us that we have failed to engage them, failed to communicate that this is something that might interest them, and that we think is going to be exciting. Conversely, the talk becomes something that is aimed entirely at preschool children with an amusing visual aid and little that speaks to adults. Effectively the adults go off into the corner to do colouring – only it happens inside their heads!

Ideally what should be happening is that the story that is unfolding in someone's life connects with the universal stories of our faiths and helps to give birth to a new story. And

> What should be happening is that the story that is unfolding in someone's life connects with the universal stories of our faiths and helps to give birth to a new story

because our lives are constantly changing, and because the ways the story is presented changes, there is an ever new stream of stories and experiences on offer. We are privileged to tell the same story over and over again in endlessly new ways. The author Michael Morpurgo writes of the experience of seeing his stories appearing in different forms: 'I love that, the transformation into a film, into an opera, into a stage play: each breathes new life, a different life, into a story.'[9] We need to love it too, the opportunity each month, or week, to re-present and reinterpret the story in different ways.

Other chapters have explored different ways of presenting the Scriptures, including using the space differently, using different voices, re-imagining into the contemporary world, offering special effects and multi-sensory experiences. Sometimes the story simply needs to stand alone, with little or no commentary. This is something our churches find very difficult.

Godly Play is an approach to Scripture and worship that has helped to open up the very real possibility of wondering together about a story and allowing each person to own a meaning and a relevance that day. The structure of a Godly Play session is the same structure as that identified earlier as the basic framework of worship – gather, listen, respond, go out. Godly Play involves creating sacred space, offering the word of God, allowing those present (of whatever age) a free response, sharing a feast, and then going out to the world. This approach to story is deeply concerned with the possibility of encounter with God rather than the goal of learning about God. See <www.godlyplay.org.uk> for more information.

However, for most churches the reading of Scripture will be followed by the talk.

Many of those faced with the challenge of an all-age talk fall into the trap of offering a children's talk. That usually means that the starting point has been one of two thoughts – either: How will I help young children understand this story? or What's a good visual aid? Sadly, it is often the second that shapes the whole all-age event. It happens to all of us.

I was outside a toy shop one day when I saw a bubble machine, and in an impetuous moment bought it, telling myself it would make a great illustration for a talk. A couple of weeks later I was doing a talk at a baptism celebration service, and decided to use the bubble machine. It's quite difficult now to remember just why I thought a bubble machine illustrated prayers . . . What I failed to realize was that toddlers think bubbles are just about the most exciting thing ever and that dissolving bubbles turn stone floors into glorious wet slides (or danger zones, depending on your perspective). Result: chaos, and no effective talk at all! (Although I do know of at least one church that uses bubbles very effectively.)

Preparing the talk for everyone

Preparing a talk for an all-age service should begin with the text itself and, if appropriate, the theme that has already been decided, for example, the new school year or the world Church or Education Sunday. But these kinds of theme do not give us the universal themes that will help everyone present to engage with the story that is being told.

The first task is to look at the readings, perhaps in the context of a predetermined theme, and see what emerges. Sometimes we need to think about the theme to help choose the readings. For example, harvest. One year, we spent sometime identifying universal themes around harvest – these included saying thank you, stewardship of creation and something about greed. This led us to the story of Zacchaeus and a retelling which involved piling boxes on top of someone until they could no longer reach out to other people in friendship. Zac became 'Billy-no-mates' until Jesus came and helped him. Then Zac gave everything away, leaving his hands free to make friends and to share. We then talked about the things that different age groups find difficult to share and ended up with three variations – one involving books and learning, one involving food and one involving friends, drawing out the idea that if we hang onto things we might not notice the needs of others.

Using universal themes

Universal themes are those things that are relevant regardless of age, status, gender, ability. They run through all kinds of stories, comedies, tragedies, adventures and travels. Some of these themes include questions such as:

- Am I loved?
- What happens when I do wrong?
- What if I fail?
- How do I love other people?
- How do I deal with fear?
- What will I do with my life?
- Am I any good at things?

> Universal themes are those things that are relevant regardless of age, status, gender, ability

Many of the best all-age communications pick up on these themes and then place them in contexts that speak to different experiences. This is something that experienced preachers do all the time. No congregation is homogeneous. Whenever I say that, I can see people's minds ticking away getting ready to challenge me. Usually someone will say that their church gathering consists only of people over 60 – a sadly familiar story in many of our churches on Sunday mornings. But a congregation of 60 years and over is not a group of homogeneous people. For example, women aged 60 to 70 are likely to have spent some or all of their life as part of the paid workforce; women over 75 less so. Adults who are aged 75 or more may have childhood memories of war, others will not. Men born before 1942 may have done National Service, those born later will not. There are so many differences across the generations, even before we begin to look at differences in life experiences.

These days it is not so easy to relate stages of life to ages of life. One of my friends, aged 54, is a grandfather of three; another of the same age is parent to two under-5s. People in our congregations may be married, childless, widowed, unwell, orphaned, unemployed . . . countless variations. Just as adults are not a single group, neither are children and young people. They too will bring the different shapes of their life experience, even if only over three, four or seven years.

A good preacher is constantly looking for illustrations and examples that will bring the universal theme to life to a wide range of individual lives. This could be by making reference to events from the past, that have resonance with the memories of one group, or it could be by using a range of contemporary cultural references. Humour is one of the ways in which this kind of multilayering is most effective.

> A good preacher is constantly looking for illustrations and examples that will bring the universal theme to life to a wide range of individual lives

Another favourite Pixar scene is from *Finding Nemo*. This film is about a father fish who loses his son (echoes of the Prodigal here) after trying too hard to keep him safe. He then sets off to find him, and on the way has a series of adventures with his new friend, Dory, a fish with memory loss. At one point they run into a group of sharks. There then follows a scene which is full of allusions to addiction recovery programmes (all the sharks are trying to resist blood: they chant, 'Fish are friends, not food') and to other films, many of which will only have been seen by adults. The scene is very funny for adults, but also remains engaging to children as they follow the characters and their behaviour. The film *Gnomeo and Juliet* is an animation based on the story of Romeo and Juliet as lived out by feuding garden gnomes, which had sections of the audience (me!) who knew Shakespeare laughing aloud at some of the allusions and asides. However, those with no knowledge at all were still engaging with the film – whether young or old.

We can use humour in sermons and talks, and it is a particularly effective way of speaking to one part of the audience alone. Asides that make reference to particular experiences of one group, usually the adults, do this very well.

✔ Tip

Humour should never be used in a way that ridicules the experiences of one group over another. Nor should laughter be used to patronize or expose children who offer answers and ideas. This is more common than it should be in our churches.

In a small church I asked the congregation to have a think about who was the most important person in the village. After an opportunity to talk to one another, I invited some ideas. A lad of about 8 or 9 was desperate to tell me, so I asked for his idea. 'The ice cream man,' he said, and all the adults laughed. The boy looked confused and uncertain. I asked him why he said that. 'Because he goes around the houses where people live and parks in the middle for the tourists,' he replied, thus identifying the tension at the heart of a small community overrun with coaches and visitors for much of the year. Shared humour can be used with great effect, but also needs to be used with great care.

Every congregation is a multi-generational congregation. It's just that sometimes we span a wider range of experiences and ages than we do at other times. Preparing an all-age talk means we have to draw on the kinds of context that are relevant to children, young adults and grandparents. Some of these contexts may have remained similar across the years. On Mothering Sunday the experience of giving and receiving presents is shared down the generations, and beginning with the memories of older people is a great way of ensuring the talk is engaging with their lives as well as with the excited children present. Mothering Sunday (or Father's Day) can be particularly challenging with congregations who have very different experiences and memories of parenting. As someone who neither has a mother nor is a mother, I have found it helpful to use the memories of gifts from the past to open up a conversation in the service. It also gives people permission to feel sad or lonely, as well as celebrating with those for whom it is a special day.

> Every congregation is a multi-generational congregation. It's just that sometimes we span a wider range of experiences and ages than we do at other times

It helps enormously to create a real cross-generational feel if older people are invited to speak before children. A recent talk about a difficult Scripture story (the Syro-Phoenician woman) began with a passion fruit. I passed it to some older people to ask if they knew what it was. And when someone guessed, I then asked if they used to eat it when they were young. A bit of reminiscence about war shortages followed, and then I invited the people to smell, look, taste the fruit. If you ask a child for input first, the adults switch off. They decide that this is a children's talk, rather than something for them as well. Children can be invited to join in very quickly, but the adults remain on side if they have been engaged early enough.

> It helps enormously to create a real cross-generational feel if older people are invited to speak before children

Likewise I never bring children to the front separately from their parents – unless I have a specific purpose which only involves them, like briefing them to go and speak to adults.

With the best will in the world, if the children are gathered at your feet, there are two likely outcomes:

- You will start to talk just to them, leaving the adults as spectators to a children's talk – which is fine if that is what you want to do.

OR

- You will ignore the children and start talking to the adults, at which point the children disengage and start fidgeting, whispering, rolling around your feet, etc. – just in the space where everyone is looking at them!

✔ Tip

If there is a need to bring children to the front, invite children and their grown-up to come to the front, or encourage children at the end of rows, nearest the centre. If you are fortunate enough to have flexible seating, it's much easier to arrange groups of seats to reflect more of a family style.

Finding the kinds of illustration, reference and example that will speak to the variety of contexts with which a congregation is familiar can be daunting. Many of those who prepare talks for all ages lack confidence in their knowledge of the world that children and parents inhabit. But being knowledgeable about their world is vital. If we want to be expert at something then part of developing that expertise is to investigate what others offer –so reading and watching contemporary media is vital. (It means watching TV becomes engaging with popular culture – a great excuse!)

Michael Morpurgo again:

> **To have read widely and deeply, to have soaked oneself in the words and ideas of other writers, to have seen what is possible and wonderful, to have listened to the music of their words and to have read the work of the masters must be a help for any writer discovering his own technique, her own voice.**[10]

Morpurgo's advice on exploring the work of others in the same field is very important. This means being aware of how others are communicating with all ages in an effective way. Ask yourself some of the questions that I have been asking.

Notice which TV programmes attract or aim to attract family audiences, and reflect on the skills of good multi-generational communicators, for example Ant and Dec. Children like Ant and Dec – they are trustworthy, empathetic, critical at times, and humorous. Adults like them for the same reasons. Another person who is brilliant at all-age communication is the radio and TV presenter Chris Evans. On his Radio 2 programmes he has often included a conversation with a child. He always treats them seriously, never patronizes or ridicules, but affirms and encourages. He is kind without being sentimental – and concerned for the well-being of the child on those occasions when the technology at either end has failed. Considering how people like this communicate is vital if we are to do the same thing in church.

We also need to be aware of the things that children and their parents are interested and engaged with. This does not mean having to watch hours of things that you personally find appalling or dull – it does, however, mean being respectful of the culture,

> **We also need to be aware of the things that children and their parents are interested and engaged with**

and taking a few moments to discover what is currently interesting. This could be as simple as checking TV listings and review pages or casting an eye over the sports page. It could also mean talking to young families about their lives and discovering what they do both together and separately at different ages. For example, we recently used the opening sequence of *In the Night Garden*, a current BBC toddler programme, as a backdrop to the idea of the calm after the storm. It is so peaceful, the boat bobbing on the sea – and deeply familiar to toddlers and young parents.

It's also important to be aware of the breadth of children's experience and awareness, otherwise we run the risk of being irrelevant and patronizing. This is particularly important if we are to engage sevens to elevens effectively in our multi-generational communication. When you are a 5-year-old your aim in life is not to be a middle-aged adult, but rather a big girl or boy. Likewise when you are 8, the next stage to admire is a teenager. Programmes and media that feature teenagers are often hugely popular with children, so checking that the examples you use are challenging and appropriate is important.

Children need to be taken seriously – don't assume they are not concerned with serious issues. When it's time for Comic Relief or Children in Need, junior-age children are some of the most engaged, not simply because of the enjoyment factor but also because they are instinctively concerned with justice. Offer children and adults a radical message of the kingdom. Leave the baby in the manger and let Jesus grow up!

In a similar way, we need not be afraid of naming painful and difficult experiences, many of which children share. Although we would like to idealize childhood as something full of sweetness and light, hope and joy, almost every child will have a range of negative experiences that cast shadows. The death of a pet is often the first encounter children have with death and, given that most younger children include their pets when identifying family, this loss is profound. But alongside that, children face family tensions, friendship difficulties and pressure around learning and school.

> **Children face family tensions, friendship difficulties and pressure around learning and school**

Several years ago a child asked me a question. He said, 'Do you always have to pretend when you go to church on Sunday?' A bit more talking and listening followed. Most of his Saturday nights were spent listening in fear to volatile arguments, often destructive, between his parents. Then on Sunday the whole family put on a smile and went to church, where there was nothing to connect the story of his life with the story of the gospel.

There are also rich resources from the past to draw on. If something has stood the test of time, it is probably worth referencing today. Classic children's books make great all-age examples – the chances are high that Granny, Dad and the children have seen and wept at *The Railway Children*[11] (although not every generation will know it as a book!). Beatrix Potter's characters, and Winnie-the-Pooh, Alice in Wonderland, more recently Harry Potter and so many more have spoken down the generations and make excellent illustrations for universal themes. There are also the films that have been mentioned several times, films worth looking at carefully, not because they are Christian or even that they can be turned into Christian tales, but simply because they are excellent stories speaking to universal themes.

Life stories

Apart from the wealth of material that can illustrate talks, there are also life's shared experiences to draw upon, whether family celebrations, life milestones or everyday occurrences like shopping, playing sport and journeys. These experiences are also some of the most powerful metaphors for the Christian life, stretching back into the Scriptures. Making the link by identifying contemporary experiences with those of long ago helps to make the stories connect, and reshape as a new story.

> **Making the link by identifying contemporary experiences with those of long ago helps to make the stories connect, and reshape as a new story**

Some of these connections are easy to make, like thinking about the boy setting off to see Jesus, carrying his packed lunch. It immediately resonates with all those school trips or family outings that have been made down the years. But there are other stories too that travel the centuries. It may be that in your context there are refugee families; hearing the real story of a family who had to flee suddenly from their home when persecution came made the story of the exodus seem very pertinent, especially when shared by an 11-year-old boy. Drawing on the real-life stories (testimonies) of the congregation is another way it is possible for everyone present to engage with the great story of God's purposes.

There are a myriad of ways to bring the talk to life, using the kind of multi-sensory approaches explored earlier, ensuring that illustrations stretch across generations and especially drawing on universal themes and stories. But the starting point is always the sacred stories and teachings, reflecting carefully on what might be the key focus for the day. Then the activities, visuals and illustrations can be brought in to serve and support the possibility. However, there is always the talk that is given and the myriad talks that are heard. This is just as true in a multi-generational context as with any other congregation. We may intend people to go away thinking about one thing, but the Holy Spirit takes the words and images and is the One who ultimately makes the connections.

To think about

- What books and films have you enjoyed that seem to cross boundaries?

- How would you go about constructing an all-age talk? Do you agree that the Scripture comes first or have you found other approaches to be valid?

- Who in your church is able to give talks and what training have they been given?

Notes

1 Robert Velarde, *The Wisdom of Pixar*, Downers Grove, Ill.: IVP, 2010, p. 9.
2 L. M. Montgomery, *Anne of Green Gables*.
3 Michael Morpurgo, *War Horse*, London: Egmont, 2007.
4 Charles Dickens, *David Copperfield*.
5 Frances Hodgson Burnett, *The Secret Garden*.
6 Ian Serraillier, *The Silver Sword*.
7 Judith Kerr, *The Tiger Who Came to Tea*, Collins Picture Lions, 1968.
8 C. S. Lewis, *The Lion, the Witch and the Wardrobe*.
9 Michael Morpurgo, *Singing for Mrs Pettigrew: Stories and Essays from a Writing Life*, Somerville, Mass.: Candlewick Press, 2007, p. 60.
10 Morpurgo, *Singing for Mrs Pettigrew*, p. 25.
11 E. Nesbit, *The Railway Children*.

5

Putting it all together

I recently attended a very ordinary church service. There were probably around 40 people there, ranging from age 3 to 90, but with the overwhelming majority in the over-55s age range. Nothing was done with the worship to make it particularly accessible to the children. The hymns were traditional, the sermon was straightforward, the prayers and readings given from the lectern. The children remained in the church throughout. They didn't even go to the special children's area at the back. They were clearly at ease in this place and they felt included. The key? The minister liked the children, smiled at them, and with every word he uttered he had an intention of including them.

In the end the best tools in the world will not make worship for whoever is present happen. After years of observation and reflection and countless training courses, I have concluded that without a deep commitment from the church to include and engage everyone, it simply won't happen.

Putting it all together is more than devising the content, more than choosing the right songs and selecting the person to speak. It is about an attitude that is held by the church and the church leadership. Worship for everyone present is not simply about adding in a few extra creative flourishes, making a few contemporary allusions and singing enthusiastically. It is about a desire and a longing in the church to be complete and to ensure that everyone has the possibility of an encounter with God, whether through offering praise and thanks, praying for those on their mind, or being challenged by the word of God.

'Everyone' is a very interesting word. It is used very casually in our everyday speech and in our church language as well. The service was drawing to a close and the notices were being given out – that mandatory part of Sunday morning gatherings! With great energy the vicar talked about the forthcoming quiz night, 8 p.m. Friday evening, everyone was really welcome. In the pews an 8-year-old bounced excitedly and whispered to her mum about how good she was at quizzes. 'Please can we go? Please?' she begged, only to hear the whispered response from her mum that the event wasn't for children. So what did the word 'everyone' mean?

Often we use the word when we mean every adult. We also do this with the word 'people'. 'How many people were in church this morning?' I asked a while ago. 'Oh, twenty-five and three children.' (The baby was left out altogether!) Children are people, not a different species!

If we are to welcome everyone into worship, then the whole church needs to cultivate an understanding that everyone matters, everyone is interesting and everyone is important. This might mean taking some time to think about what we think is happening for children and adults when they come to church. As stated earlier, for many years the Church has subconsciously carried an educational model into church, particularly in regard to the presence of children and adults together. This means that we think of church as a kind of school – a place where

> If we are to welcome everyone into worship, then the whole church needs to cultivate an understanding that everyone matters, everyone is interesting and everyone is important

children learn about God, learn how to behave and learn how to worship. They may do this in all kinds of engaging ways, but the underlying assumptions mean that children are seen as the recipients of what is on offer, and a few adults have a particular responsibility to make this happen. Many churches invite children to the front after they return from peer groups so they can show the congregation what it is they have been doing. At its best this can be a moment of real engagement and sharing, but very often it is about reassuring ourselves that the children are 'learning something'. The questions we ask children after church are framed in terms of what information or knowledge has been taken on board. There is little expectation that children are going to encounter God (there may be little expectation for anyone present!).

I was once in a shopping mall when we realized that a TV celebrity was there. The children were immediately energized and excited. We pressed into the gathering crowd of all ages, all equally enthusiastic. It wasn't even anyone especially well-known, but the possibility of encounter had sent a thrill through many. Adults were helping children to get a better view and doing that wonderfully British thing of talking to each other – a thing we do in times of crisis and times of excitement. Imagine this kind of enthusiastic energy as we approached church! Children are not being brought to a learning opportunity – the whole family, the whole people of God are gathering for the possibility of an encounter with God!

> Children are not being brought to a learning opportunity – the whole family, the whole people of God are gathering for the possibility of an encounter with God!

To have this kind of welcome to a service where everyone is included means that the congregation is glad when there is a real diversity present. I'm always struck by how much a baby or a toddler impacts a family gathering. Sometimes it's a new arrival, sometimes it's a reunion after a time of absence, but whatever the reason there is such delight in seeing a baby. The same thing used to happen at our mid-week communion service. A young mum started to attend with her baby, later with her toddler and second baby. Our little group of well-retired men

and women smiled more, relaxed and were so glad to see them. A child in our midst is a blessing and should gladden everyone's heart.

Roles and responsibilities

Although the whole church needs to think about how we can embrace whoever is present, there are those with particular responsibilities. Welcomers, refreshment teams, musicians, readers and others might need to think about their part in creating the possibility of engagement and worship. But a particular responsibility falls on the worship leader – or leaders.

In the early part of the novel *To the Lighthouse*,[1] Mrs Ramsey hosts a dinner party. There is a wonderful description of how for a moment she feels the whole weight of responsibility resting with her. She has drawn these people together, and it is she who will draw the threads together and weave the evening into a pattern. Thankfully, when we lead a service, it is God who stands alongside us, the Holy Spirit who breathes life into thoughts and feelings, transforming them into encounters and prayers. However, there is also a very real sense in which the minister has to hold all things together. The words of the service are like a script – those who will deliver it are the ones who will make it live. A good script helps enormously, but bad actors can make even the greatest drama unintelligible, as can those who are unprepared and unrehearsed.

> The words of the service are like a script – those who will deliver it are the ones who will make it live

✔ Tip

The all-age service on Sunday (or other occasion) is the tip of an iceberg. It is the visible result of a whole range of thinking and planning that has been going on.

Some of that preparing will be the ongoing reflection about what it means to be a church that welcomes and includes everyone. Some of it is in the commitment to prayer.

There is the task of planning for all-age worship. Many churches offer a specifically all-age-focused service once a month. In my dream church, all worship would be worship for whoever is present, and certainly the attitude of inclusion and welcome needs to be present at every gathering. Some churches are so surprised when a family with a couple of young children appears on a Sunday, that they inadvertently start with a negative: 'Gosh! We never expected you to be here today! We don't have any children's activities today, so you might find it a bit boring!' This is a complete contrast to the kind of greeting offered at a secular all-age activity, where the norm is to anticipate that people want to be there and that what is on offer will be a positive experience. Try saying something more like: 'It's great to see you! There is so much to look at in this church, the stones breathe history and the words are inspiring. If you need any help just ask us.'

Planning ahead

On the Sunday designated as 'all-age Sunday' there is (hopefully) a good culture of welcome. But long before the appointed day publicity needs to happen and a programme needs to be decided.

✔ Tip

Planning for a year is a good idea. Take time to look through the year ahead and decide themes for each Sunday, choose which festivals to celebrate and pencil in any special events. Be realistic. If you are growing a family congregation from nothing, it is better to have two good family events in the year than to try to put on something in every school holiday.

The outlines in this book give you a theme for each month of the year within an overall theme of 'something for everyone'. This might give you a good starting point for the year, although in some months it may be more appropriate to celebrate a festival (see the companion volume to this one, *Festivals Together*).

Publicizing your services

When you have a plan for the year, then you can begin to think about publicity. So often a huge amount of energy is put into planning a special all-age service.

When the day comes there are a handful of faithful people, and perhaps one or two families with links to the church. Spirits fall and disappointment sets in as people wonder why the community haven't flocked in. Unfortunately, a poster in the village shop and a leaflet in the book bag may not be enough.

Effective advertising

The most effective way I have found of slowly building a family congregation is through the baptism register and invitations sent month after month to these families. If possible, use the post, and hand-address them. There is nothing more exciting – and rare – these days than a proper letter with a stamp and handwriting dropping through the letter box. Slowly this builds up a sense of involvement. People would stop me in the village shop and apologize for not coming. After a while I realized that some felt connected to the church even if they were yet to make it on a Sunday. It is slow work, but worthwhile. This kind of approach is then supported by posters and other publicity. If you have a worked-out programme, it's a good idea to print out dates and themes for six months and send that out to families so they can keep it to hand.

The themes in this book are all based around lectionary themes with suggested readings taken from the readings at that point in the year. Themes can be generated in all kinds of ways, but using the lectionary is a very good place to start. It widens the biblical material that we consider – and is sometimes very challenging. However, if there is a specific focus to the all-age gatherings – for example, attracting those with little Christian background – it may be appropriate to devise a series of themes around basic beliefs or around the Lord's Prayer.

✔ Tip

Choosing themes

All-age services often attract those less familiar with church, and it might be important to connect to the themes and events that matter to families rather than those that matter to the church. Including occasions like Valentine's Day, Father's Day, Children in Need, helps to build bridges to family life.

Rehearsing your service

Once a theme is in place, the hard work of preparing for a particular service begins. This book contains a series of prepared outlines, and there are many others available. But unfortunately you can't just pick up the outline on Saturday evening and go with it. There is a big difference between a first read-through of a script and a performance! The outline needs to be looked at, ideas developed that will work in the local context, and tasks allocated, including the sourcing of any resources needed. And, where necessary, there needs to be a rehearsal. This is something churches skip all too often.

We decide to do a dramatic reading of Jesus stilling the storm. Scripts are handed out as people arrive on Sunday morning, usually three minutes before the service. There is little time to do more than glance at the words. When the moment for the 'dramatic reading' happens, the biggest drama is the pause before each line is spoken, and a serious Gospel reading becomes unintentionally humorous.

If you are the worship leader or minister, it is also worth checking out the logistics and mechanics of any activity that involves movement around the space. Think about how people will move from their seats and return to them and where anything that is to be collected will be positioned. If you are using new readers, of whatever age, take time to practise using a microphone or, if you are in a church without a sound system, practise where will be the best place to stand. (If you do have a sound system, insist on using it! It makes a huge difference to those with hearing difficulties and also in helping children engage with what is happening.)

Choosing and using music

Music is an important part of our worship, and plays a big role in helping different people encounter God. There have been many changes in the way we access music over the past few years, and popular music can seem a long way removed from the music played in church. Singing also happens much less in schools than it used to, although programmes like *The Big Sing* have tried to address this and reintroduce communal singing to school groups. A recent surge of interest in adult choirs (*Rock Choir*, etc.) and in the

US concept of the 'show choir' (as seen on *Glee*) are also helping to reignite an interest in choral singing as well as performance.

For many younger families, public singing is a daunting prospect, and it can be valuable to include music to listen to as well as traditional hymn-singing. If you are fortunate enough to have an alternative to the organ, this can really change the tone and style of a service. In one church a set of drums and a keyboard changed the family service, simply by adding a more informal relaxed tone. We still sang the same hymns, but slowly introduced some more contemporary songs.

Generally, we need to offer far fewer hymns over time than we think. Most people enjoy singing things they know well, so repetition builds confidence. Add in new things slowly and repeat often in the first few months. It's also good to sing new words to familiar tunes (always better than the other way round!) – but this is not very easy for those who cannot read.

If it's possible to put words on a screen, it changes the way people sing. They sing up and out instead of entertaining the floor and the back of the person in front.

When using music to support words or to support a time of reflection, whether seated or moving, think carefully about the ambience and the mood. And always check the whole lyrics of a song – an inappropriate word might pass unnoticed in your living room, but blasting out into the silence of church is a different matter!

Music is also one of the ways in which people of all ages can take part in leading worship. Traditional choirs can be a great way of encouraging children and young people to take their place alongside adults as part of leading worship, as can serving. It's easy to overlook the role of children in these activities. I've heard adults express disappointment that there were no children present at a service, completely ignoring those in the choir or at the Communion table. It may also be possible to include children and adults together in a music group, if you have the right person to develop their skills. The leadership of such initiatives is vital, but if you have a passion and skill in the church, the outcome is often very effective. Some churches develop children's choirs, others develop drama groups.

It is also worth thinking about creating a dance group, which might even incorporate gymnastics. One church created routines to contemporary worship songs using dance movements and solo gymnastic skills, all of which helped children to feel part of what was happening.

It is important that these kinds of activity are worship and not performance. Working with children, young people and adults together is also about developing gifts and skills for leadership and ministry, not just a chance to demonstrate they are good at something. Everything should be part of helping those present worship God.

There are also other ways of involving children, but any task or role given to them needs to be given with real intention and expectation of their ability, otherwise it too easily becomes patronizing. In one church, some 11-year-old boys took on responsibility for the Fairtrade stall. They put out the table and the stock, became salespeople and counted the money, with oversight from an adult, but with real responsibility. Children can be assistant sidespeople, readers, intercessors and be involved in other ways. By the age of 16 a young person is eligible to be on the PCC – involvement in the life of the church helps people to own what is happening and feel a real sense of belonging.

From the moment the minister says, 'The Lord be with you', the process of inclusion begins.

Leading worship for everyone present means that the word 'you' has to encompass the whole range of people who are there. It's about who is being called to mind and being mindful of them. For some people this is instinctive and unconscious – others need to become aware of who they are addressing when they begin the worship service. And there is nothing that helps so much as a smile and eye contact. In some church traditions this is rare, but if we want to create the kind of worship that is broad in appeal, there needs to be a more relaxed approach. The power of a smile is amazing.

The power of a smile is amazing

After one very, very formal nine lessons and carols service, a woman approached me to talk. She told me that she knew I would be friendly. I couldn't figure out how in a service where every step and every word had been pre-planned she could possibly have singled me out as an approachable person. But apparently I smiled as we walked out in procession – a tiny moment of informality that spoke volumes to her.

The style of accessible all-age worship needs to be 'intentional informal'. It is intentional because we have a serious purpose. We want everyone present to encounter God. We want to give glory to his name, and offer our sacrifice of praise. We want to hear his word and be encouraged to live out our lives of discipleship. All of this is serious – and intentional. But we can also be relaxed, putting people at their ease, holding lightly to some of the formalities of our traditions. Worship is not an intellectual activity, though we may use our minds. Ultimately, worship is about relationships: our relationship with God, with each other and with the world around. The possibility of human relationship is modelled in the way the leader(s) connect(s) with the members of the congregation, respecting them and including them. Smiling really helps! One of the reasons we smile is because we are enjoying ourselves, and that kind of enjoyment is infectious. If those leading worship can communicate in tone, gesture and words that they are glad to be there, then the whole gathering grows in confidence and anticipation.

Ultimately, worship is about relationships: our relationship with God, with each other and with the world around

Leaders have to be confident and expectant, especially when introducing new approaches to things. Imagine the scene. A minister begins to speak: 'Now, I know lots of you prefer to sit still, but we have got children here, and it's nice for the children to do something, so if you don't mind, and I know some of you do, we're going to stand up and stretch high, aren't we children?' It's a caricature, I know, but the conviction with which things are introduced and explained is important.

If an activity is described in terms of the children, not only will the adults become uncertain about whether to participate, but most of the older children will decide it's not for them. Clear instructions are important, which often require some planning and preparation, and a real sense that this activity is part of the worship. If an activity involves movement which some may find awkward, offer an alternative, but in a way that is helpful rather than an easy excuse not to join in.

Expectations need to be realistic. We often put far more pressure on the congregation at all-age or family services than we do on other regular congregations. On the Sunday before my Mum's funeral I went to the parish church in my home town. The first hymn was 'Be thou my vision', and for a whole range of reasons it was a very moving and inspiring hymn for me that day. I can't tell you what the readings were, what the sermon was about, or that God met with me in the prayers or the bread and wine. But I did encounter God thanks to that hymn. The service is not a failure because only one thing spoke to me – in fact, the minister was glad that I had found it so helpful.

We don't expect every adult to find every part of the service equally engaging, yet somehow when everyone present includes children we start to put pressure on both the liturgy and those attending to be equally and universally engaged with every part of the service. A baby, child or adult might leave worship thinking about the way the sun made colours fall onto the floor of the church, one of those things that frequently speaks to people of

God in ways beyond words. Another person might find their attention caught by a line in a reading, leading them to think about a situation in their lives. Some days there may be nothing at all that stands out. Simply being there is enough. And that is okay. Putting the worship together is about the possibility of encounter – but the Holy Spirit moves through and beyond the things we do, stirring hearts in unexpected ways.

> Some days there may be nothing at all that stands out. Simply being there is enough. And that is okay

When you have finally put together all that is going to happen in the worship service, take some time to review the whole programme. A good practice is to call to mind one or two people who might be attending, and ask yourself:

- Is there something that has the potential to help 80-year-old Mrs B worship?
- What about 6-year-old Jake?
- Is there too much movement or too much sitting down?
- Are all the songs remarkably similar?
- Is there a variety of pace, tone and energy through the overall service?

These kinds of review question are really important, and you might find a planning sheet helpful. Then when it's all over, and you are feeling really positive, take time to review it all again. Find out what works well in your context, which ideas take wings with the congregation and which seem to fall to the floor. All this builds the confidence and expertise needed to create genuine worship for everyone present.

Note

1 Virginia Woolf, *To the Lighthouse*.

Part 2

The service outlines

How to use the service outlines

The outlines that follow are ready to be used. They are designed to fit into a traditional Sunday morning worship slot and build on the principles outlined. They are not dependent on the presence of children to make them work, but rather designed to help everyone present into worship. You can use them as they are or use them as jumping-off points. If you have never done anything creative in worship before, it's possible to take one section alone and use it. For example, you might decide to introduce a creative way of leading intercessions or a new approach to presenting a reading.

Many churches have a practice of designating one service a month as a 'family' or 'all-age' service, and the outlines in this book are suitable for this kind of service. However, my dream is to create worship that works for whoever is present, and for every gathering to be for all God's people, at whatever age and stage of life they might be. It may therefore be appropriate to use some or all of these outlines for occasions not designated 'all-age'. All the outlines work within a formal liturgical structure, although they will also work in more informal settings, so it might be an opportunity to take a risk and do something differently.

The outlines are built around the structure talked about earlier. These notes should be read in conjunction with the worship outlines.

NB: If you prepare a service sheet you need to think carefully about how much to include, bearing in mind that many younger attenders will not be able to read. Where there are instructions about movement and actions, these need to be demonstrated and led by the worship leader or other appropriate person.

Title

Each month has been given a title, which informs the choice of activities and the approach to the content. The outlines are undated and therefore can be used in any given year or on any Sunday of the month. The themes arise from an overview of the lectionary across whole months and for three lectionary years – this means that the activities, talks, prayers, etc. should be appropriate when specific lectionary readings are used.

Lectionary

The choice of readings is indicative, taken from the time of year. You will need to use the appropriate readings from the authorized lectionary, although at certain times of the year the Church of England allows some freedom of choice (Ordinary Time). During the seasons of Advent, Epiphany and Easter the recommended lectionary readings must be used.

You will need

This section lists the items you will need to source for the worship suggestions. It is a good idea to build up a store of items that are used frequently, and at the end of this section there are some suggestions as to where some items can be sourced.

WE GATHER

Make a note of any suggestions for movement during the opening hymn. There are also suggestions if anything needs to be handed out before the service begins.

Opening hymn

I suggest choosing a robust, well-known all-age hymn as the first hymn. If you expect a significant number of those unfamiliar with church, choose those hymns that are lodged within the national psyche (e.g. 'Praise my soul the King of heaven') and be mindful of the hymns that parents would have known from school (e.g. 'Lord of the dance'; 'One more step'). The music needs to be appropriate for whoever is present – remembering that the wordiness of most hymns precludes non-readers from joining in anyway. A good strong tune where the rhythm can be felt by preschoolers is very helpful.

Please note that instructions about movement are in *italics*.

Opening praise/worship

Where a 'voice' is suggested, this can be anyone of any age and does not need to be an authorized minister.

We say sorry

Within the Church of England only authorized forms of confession and absolution can be used. All the suggestions in this book conform with this expectation. If a lay person is leading the service they should use the inclusive 'us' form of the absolution.

Making connections

The words spoken by/given to the minister are suggestions for linking or introducing the worship activities, and are set in a panel. Please feel free to adapt these words or to be impromptu as appropriate.

The Gloria or hymn

There are many settings of the Gloria to familiar tunes. It is important that the congregation becomes familiar with the tune and words used or, if there is a choir, this might be an opportunity for the congregation to listen to something fresh. The Gloria is not used during Lent or Advent.

The collect or prayer for the day

In the Church of England the collect for the day must be used at the principal service of the day and in those seasons where the authorized lectionary must be used. In a 'service of the word' other collects can be written, and *New Patterns of Worship* (Church House Publishing, 2008) gives suggestions for writing your own. Many of the prayers in this book are specially written or selected and are not the collect of the day.

 ## WE LISTEN

There are suggestions for presenting readings, and sometimes specific versions or adaptations of a reading are recommended. There are also some original scripts. Remember to rehearse any dramatic versions and to practise reading. If you are using more than one reading, don't do elaborate things with each reading. Keep one or two simple, and use just one in a different form.

If you are using only one reading, it must be the Gospel at a Eucharist in the Church of England.

The talk

This is a suggestion for an all-age talk based on the readings and theme. It can be used as a 'jumping-off point' and should be adapted in the light of specific lectionary readings.

Opening hymn

Many services will include a hymn or song somewhere in this part of the service. In a formal service it may be known as a 'gradual hymn' (but many church attenders have no idea what this word means, and it should be avoided for all-age services). This hymn should be a shorter, more direct hymn that reflects the readings.

 ## WE RESPOND

We believe

Each outline offers a suggestion for a creed or affirmation of faith. This has to be included in a Church of England principal service on a Sunday but is not essential in a service of the word. The form used must be authorized, and the majority of the outlines in this book use the same form each time. This is to help build a sense of familiarity and belonging, but it is appropriate to use an alternative, particularly during special seasons of the church year. There is also a 'making connections' suggestion which can be adapted as an introduction.

Prayer ideas

Most outlines contain two creative ways of praying, one of which will be static, word-based and simpler, while the other may involve movement. Sometimes these will require preparation beforehand, for example creating prayer stations, and providing objects or materials for people to use.

The prayers can be led by one or more voices, and handing the ideas to a family or a prayer group so they can prepare can be a good way of developing skills and involving more people in leading intercessions. Sometimes the prayers involve movement, and it is a good idea to have one person directing and modelling the movements while someone else says the words. If the prayer activity involves people moving around the worship space, it is helpful to play suitable music. This could be played by a worship group or organist, but it is also an opportunity to use recorded music. This needs to be selected with care. If there are lyrics then they will need to complement the prayer focus rather than distract, and the mood of the piece needs to complement the mood of the prayers. If people are being encouraged to think about sadness then blasting out: 'Oh Lord, I wanna sing your praises!' is jarring, but equally playing a haunting melody when the focus is on praying for joy in various situations may be distracting.

Although this book contains different ideas and approaches for each month, in reality you will find that certain approaches to prayer work well in specific contexts. Some congregations find prayer stations impossible, others really enjoy them. Likewise some worship leaders find they have a gift for encouraging movement in prayer, whereas others find the use of objects to be helpful. Doing something new and exciting every time is not the key to good

inclusive worship, so don't feel obliged to keep introducing different ideas. Find a few ways that work and stick with them for a while, then maybe introduce something different for a special occasion.

If the service is a service of the word, it is appropriate to end the prayers with the Lord's Prayer.

The peace

Although not essential in a non-eucharistic service, exchanging the peace is a lovely moment of inclusion and acknowledging that we are gathered as the whole people of God. Various words can be used to introduce the peace, but the formal words, 'The peace of the Lord be always with you', must be included and said by an authorized minister.

We celebrate

There are no specific suggestions offered in the outlines for the Eucharist, although it is recommended that Prayer D is used (or one of the new eucharistic prayers for use with children present, once authorized) and that thought is given to the mechanics of distribution as well as the prayers (see Chapter 3).

It is also good to involve children and adults together in bringing the gifts to the altar and also in preparing the table. A hymn is usually sung while this is happening, and it needs to be of sufficient length to allow for all the activity to take place.

WE GO OUT

This section has ideas for sending out, and alternative blessing prayers. Sometimes the dismissal involves handing things out to people, so it is important to have prepared this. As with earlier sections, where it says 'voice', any person can take part. Blessings should be said by an authorized minister, and those offered in this book are suggestions. There are many options available.

Final hymn

As with the opening hymn, it's good to choose something that has a strong, familiar tune. The first impression and the last impression are very important, so it's good if people leave feeling positive. The music will also need to fit with the style of the service – 'You shall go out with joy' may be great with an informal ending, but less suitable for a formal exit where a more traditional style will be more suitable.

Whether you decide to use these ideas and themes, or to create your own, the intention is to create the kind of worship where each person leaves feeling excited or moved by all that has happened. Each member of the church family and the domestic family feels positive about their experience. And at the next 'all-age service' the people are coming down the path full of anticipation, glad to be coming to church, knowing that there will be something welcoming and relevant happening.

Where to source things

- *Pebbles and decorative items* Stores such as Ikea, Dunelm Mill, Wilkinsons and local discount stores are good for such items.
- *Silk flowers* As above, also markets.

- *Paper hearts* Pre-cut are available from craft retailers such as Hobbycraft, and also through Baker Ross and similar online companies.
- *Map of the world* A good large plastic map is available from Early Learning Centre, and lots of toy shops sell similar items. There are specialist online map stores.
- *Confetti* Different types of shiny confetti are available in most card shops, specialist party stores and in local markets.
- *Fabric* Try local Asian fabric stores, markets or Dunelm Mill. Sheer fabrics are good as are lining materials – buy lengths of around five metres as this drapes well over tables, pulpits, etc. and is a good length for moving around the church.
- *Ribbons* Markets, haberdashers, etc.
- Many areas of the country have local authority *scrap-stores* – places that sell recyclable materials from local manufacturers to charities, schools and community groups. You can usually fill a shopping trolley for around £15. These places are not so good for specific items and quantities at short notice, but worth browsing to build up a stock of potentially useful items.
- *DIY stores* are also full of useful things!

January

A gift for everyone

This outline uses the Epiphany readings as a starting point, but could be used on any Sunday in January. Throughout the season of Epiphany the readings are always widening the vision of who Jesus is and widening the scope of his mission and ministry.

Key lectionary readings

Please see note in Chapter 6, How to use the service outlines. Epiphany is a season that requires the set lectionary readings for the day in a Church of England principal service.

Isaiah 60.1–6 'Overwhelmed by the possibilities'

Psalm 72.10–15 'For the rich and the poor'

Ephesians 3.1–12 'To make everyone see'

Matthew 2.1–12 'Two kings and some magi'

You will need

- A large gold star
- Packages to represent gifts of the magi
- A small gift box
- A crown
- Three tables with a heap of gold chocolate coins and a bowl; a scented candle or grains of incense; and perfumed oil suitable for skin contact, respectively; OR something to symbolize gold, incense, perfume

 WE GATHER

Opening hymn

During this hymn make a procession with people representing the four corners of the world behind a large gold star. Include some children carrying packages to represent gifts.

Informal welcome

Formal introduction

Minister The Lord be with you.

All **And also with you.**

Four voices speak from four different parts of the congregation OR those in the procession speak these words at the front. The whisperers could be some seated adults/children. The words can be accompanied by actions if led by those at the front.

Voice 1 We come from the East to worship the Lord.

Voice 2 We come from the North to worship the Lord.

Voice 3 We come from the West to worship the Lord.

Voice 4 We come from the South to worship the Lord.

Whisperers We come from all creation to worship the Lord.

Voices together Everyone come and worship the Lord.

All **Worship the Lord . . .** (*make hands into fists at shoulder level, facing forward, and lower to waist height*).

Voices . . . and praise his name!

All **And praise his name!** (*open palms wide and quickly raise both arms outwards above head height*)

We say sorry

Making connections

Minister Sometimes we forget that Jesus came for everyone and we forget to tell people the good news of his light and love. A small gift box is being passed through the congregation. As each of you receives it, hold it quietly for two seconds – counting to two in your heads – then pass it on, remembering the times you have forgotten to share.

(Depending on the size of the congregation you may need two or several boxes.)

While the box is being passed:

Voice   Sometimes we forget that Jesus is a gift to each of us and sometimes we ignore him in our lives. Lord, have mercy.

All   Lord, have mercy.

Voice   Sometimes we forget that Jesus came for everyone and we ignore those who we don't like. Christ, have mercy.

All   Christ, have mercy.

Voice   Sometimes we forget that we need to tell others the good news of God's love and we keep it to ourselves. Lord, have mercy.

All   Lord, have mercy.

Minister   May the God of all healing and forgiveness
           draw *us* to himself,
           and cleanse *us* from all *our* sins
           that we may behold the glory of his Son,
           the Word made flesh,
           Jesus Christ our Lord.

All   Amen.[1]

Hymn/Gloria

Collect or prayer for the day

See note in Chapter 6, How to use the service outlines.

Minister   God of all,
           You sent Jesus as a gift for all the world
           and you send us to share that gift with others;
           give us courage to speak
           and wisdom to act
           so that we and all the world
           will know that Jesus is Lord
           Amen.

 WE LISTEN

Reading(s)

You will need to act out a tableau representing the magi arriving to see Jesus. While this is happening, someone goes into the pulpit or to another vantage point in the church, unrolls a scroll and reads the words from Isaiah.

If you are doing this after the feast of the Epiphany, you could simply use the Isaiah reading without the tableau.

Talk

Place someone big and powerful on your left (representing Herod).

Place a timid-looking family holding an older baby on your right (representing Jesus and the Holy Family).

Hold up a crown.

Then talk in the manner of a boxing intro.

Speaker   On my left we have Contender Number One, the first king in our story. He's big, he's brave, he's bold. (*Herod struts about a bit.*) He wants power and he wants to win. He knows what being a king is all about. What's it about, Herod?

Herod   'It's all about me! (*Points to himself and gets everyone to chant back: 'It's all about me!' etc.*)

Speaker   But on my right we have Contender Number Two, the second king in our story. He's little, he's tiny, he's . . . he's a baby! He wants . . . well, what does he want? How can we know? He's just a baby.

Parents hold up baby and say timidly   Well, we think it's all about you . . .

Speaker   So the contest is between all about me, and all about you. (*End mini-contest.*)

Ask people to talk to each other about the two slogans. What kind of person might each of them be? Get some feedback. Say something similar to:

Two thousand years ago the Jewish people were waiting for a leader, a Messiah to save them. They thought he would come just for them. They thought he would come with a big show of power and might.

The story of Jesus that unfolds is one where we begin to realize that Jesus is a bigger king than anyone ever guessed . . . and he's a different kind of king. This is a king who says to each and every human person . . . it's all about YOU.

I wonder how many people fit into your house. How many people could fit in to see Jesus? There were Mum, Dad, the magi and all their servants. But then it seems there is room for (*start inviting people from congregation out to the front*) you, and you, and you, and you (*gather more and more, crowding into the space*) there is room for all of us here, for all who live in our village, our county, our country, and our world . . .

> Jesus has come for YOU, and for everyone.
>
> That's what we need to hear as Christmas fades away. We need to remind ourselves that Jesus came for YOU, for everyone.

 **WE RESPOND**

Creed or statement of faith

Making connections

Minister We've thought about God's promise – the love that reaches to everyone. So let's stand and speak out together what we believe:

All **We believe in God the Father,**
from whom every family
in heaven and on earth is named.

We believe in God the Son,
who lives in our hearts through faith,
and fills us with his love.

We believe in God the Holy Spirit,
who strengthens us
with power from on high.

We believe in one God;
Father, Son and Holy Spirit.
Amen.[2]

Prayers

EITHER 'Bearing gifts of prayer'

Place three tables in church, either together at front, or at different accessible places.

- Table 1 to have a heap of gold chocolate coins and an empty bowl. Invite people to place a coin into the bowl and as they do to pray for people with power and wealth in the world.

- Table 2 to have some incense burning or scented candles to light. Invite people to either place some grains of incense into the burner or light a candle as their prayer for the Church in the world.

- Table 3 to have some perfumed oil suitable for skin contact. Invite people to make the sign of the cross on their own hands or the hands of someone else as they pray for those who are struggling, suffering or sad.

Each table could also have some specific appropriate themes on card.

While this is happening, play some music, e.g. from Taizé.

When everyone is finished, the leader offers a short gathering prayer in these or similar words:

> Gracious God, whose love reaches out to everyone, famous or unknown, rich or poor, healthy or unwell, happy or sad, we ask you to hear all the prayers of our hearts this day, in Jesus' name, Amen.

OR 'Gifts for the world'

These prayers can be led more formally but using different voices and visual symbols.

Voice 1 Gold (*hold up a symbol of gold*). The colour of gold makes us think of wealth and power. We pray today for all those in the world who make decisions that affect other people, for those who lead in this country and in our world. Help them to remember that power and authority is not about them, but is about working towards love and justice for everyone.
Lord, hear our prayer,

All **Please.**

Voice 2 Frankincense (*wave some incense or light a scented candle*). The perfume of incense makes us think of worship and the life of the Church. We pray today for the Church here and throughout the world, asking God to help us be brave in sharing the good news of love to everyone around us.
Lord, hear our prayer,

All **Please.**

Voice 3 Myrrh (*hold up a symbol of perfume*). The richness of myrrh reminds us of times of sadness. We pray today for all those we know who are struggling with life for whatever reason, and we pray that those who help them will have wisdom and compassion to share God's love with them.
Lord, hear our prayer,

All **Please.**

(Finally, invite people to place their hands over their own hearts.)

Leader We give thanks that we have been included in the love of God and invited to follow Jesus. We pray that we will have the courage to be faithful each day and to share that love within our workplace, our school, our community, our families.

If the service is a service of the word, it may be appropriate to end the prayers with the

Lord's Prayer, before sharing the peace together. If the service is a Eucharist, continue with the peace followed by the bringing of gifts, the preparing of the table and the eucharistic prayer. Involve different generations as appropriate.

The peace

Introduce the peace, using these or similar words:

Minister   Christ came and proclaimed the gospel:

   peace to those who are far off
   and peace to those who are near.

   The peace of the Lord be always with you.

All   **And also with you.**[3]

 **WE GO OUT**

Notices may be included at this point as part of moving the focus to our Christian lives.

Voice 1   We carry the light of hope to the West/East/ North/South . . . (*turning to different directions*)

All   **and share it with a waiting world.**
Voice 2   We carry the word of life . . .
All   **and share it with a waiting world.**
Voice 3   We carry God's heart of love . . .
All   **and share it with a waiting world.**

Blessing

Minister   May the peace of the Christ-child
      be in your homes,
   may the glory of the Christ-child
      shine in your heart,
   and the blessing of God,
      Father, Son and Holy Spirit
   be with you this day and always.
   Amen.

Notes

1 *New Patterns for Worship*, London: Church House Publishing, 2008, p. 97, B79.
2 *New Patterns for Worship*, p. 166, E12.
3 *New Patterns for Worship*, p. 73, H16.

Love for everyone

This outline uses the Ordinary Time after Epiphany as a starting point, but could be used on any Sunday in February. At this time of year, the readings focus on Jesus' relationship with the disciples and their growing understanding of his full identity.

Key lectionary readings

Please see note in Chapter 6, How to use the service outlines.

2 Kings 5.1–14 'I'd do anything for love'

Psalm 36.5–10 'God's love is amazing'

1 Corinthians 13 'That's what love looks like'

Mark 1.29–39 'Love into action' (or Mark 2.1–2 'What friends are for')

You will need

- Enough ripped red hearts for everyone
- Objects for talk including photo of partner; photo of child; packet of seeds; model of house; mp3 player; bag to put them in
- Lengths of ribbon or fabric in yellow, red, green, white
- Love Hearts or similar sweets to give away

 ## WE GATHER

Opening hymn

Informal welcome

Formal introduction

Minister	The Lord be with you.
All	**And also with you.**

Voice	Who do we praise?
All	**Jesus, Jesus, Jesus!** *(from quiet to loud shout)*
Voice	Who do we thank?
All	**Jesus, Jesus, Jesus!** *(from quiet to loud shout)*
Voice	Who do we love?
All	**Jesus, Jesus, Jesus!** *(from quiet to loud shout)*
Voice	Who shall we tell?
All	**Little people, big people, everybody!**

We say sorry

Making connections

Minister	Jesus commanded us to love God and to love our neighbour. But it's easy to forget. Sometimes we ourselves fall out with people, and sometimes we ignore God in our lives. Sometimes people are hurt and broken when love fades away. As the music plays, come forward and place one of the ripped hearts on the altar/table as a sign of your sadness today for your own lack of love and for the lack of love in our world.

Play music as this happens, e.g. 'All for the love' by Beth Neilson Chapman or 'Amazing grace' by Neil Diamond.

When everyone has finished:

Minister	God of mercy,
	we acknowledge that we are all sinners.
	We turn from the wrong that we have thought
	  and said and done,
	and are mindful of all that we have failed
	  to do.
	For the sake of Jesus, who died for us,
	forgive us for all that is past,
	and help us to live each day
	in the light of Christ our Lord

All	**Amen.**[1]

Minister   May the God of love
          bring *us* back to himself,
          forgive *us* *our* sins,
          and assure *us* of his eternal love
          in Jesus Christ our Lord.

All   **Amen.**[2]

Hymn/Gloria

Collect or prayer for the day

See note in Chapter 6, How to use the service outlines.

Minister   God of love,
          who loves everything that you have made,
          help us to love our friends, our family and our world,
          with the love that you showed us
          in Jesus Christ your Son,
          Amen.

 **WE LISTEN**

Reading(s)

If using only one reading, use 1 Corinthians 13.

Use a contemporary or alternative version.

If using the second Gospel suggested, it could be acted out or retold through a conversation with the congregation as it is so well known.

Talk

Family fortunes

You will need a large bag with five items inside. Suggest: photo of husband/wife; photo of child; packet of seeds (garden); model of house (home), mp3 player (music).

Invite two teams to come and take part and guess the items in the bag that people named when asked to name something they love.

Say something similar to:

> Love is a strange word. We use it for all kinds of things – from food (McDonald's slogan) through to something deep, personal and permanent – children, partners, pets, God . . .

Love can sometimes seem easy – all pink hearts and fluffy toys (*show some of this kind of item*).
But that doesn't seem to be what Paul was writing about or what Jesus came to show us.

Real love seems like hard work – Jesus spent time being with people, listening to them, healing them – even when he was tired. He knew he had to keep on telling them the good news of God's love – a love that keeps on going. Paul listed some of the qualities of love (*pick out a few of them, perhaps asking people which they remember and which seem easy or hard*).

Love keeps going through all things – love lasts for ever. In the movie *Toy Story 3*, the toys' love for Andy means that they will do everything they can to get back to him – and it is Andy's love for the toys that means he passes them on to someone else who will love them too.

Jesus showed us what love is like – and he showed us how much God loves us.

He showed us that even when people are different or difficult, God keeps on showing love, amazing love. (*Ask people for images to describe that love.*)

When we know we are loved, it becomes easier to share that love with other people – it will flow out from us to those around us and out into the world, making a difference and bringing new life to all.

 **WE RESPOND**

Creed or statement of faith

Making connections

Minister   We've thought about love that reaches to everyone. So let's stand and speak out together what we believe:

All   **We believe in God the Father,
          from whom every family
          in heaven and on earth is named.**

          **We believe in God the Son,
          who lives in our hearts through faith,
          and fills us with his love.**

          **We believe in God the Holy Spirit,
          who strengthens us
          with power from on high.**

          **We believe in one God;
          Father, Son and Holy Spirit.
          Amen.**[3]

Prayers

The colours of love

Invite young people to walk through the congregation with ribbons/banners or lengths of fabric in the colours. Give people a few moments to look at the colours before each section begins.

Voice 1   Yellow is the colour of joy.
Dear God, we give you thanks for all the wonderful things we love – for sunshine and beaches, ice cream and teddy bears. We thank you for the joy of being loved by our family and our friends. Help us to share love with other people and to be those who bring joy to others.
Lord, hear our prayer,

All   **Please.**

Voice 2   Red is the colour of hurting.
Dear God, we pray for all those who are struggling today because relationships have gone wrong. We pray for those who are angry and those who are hurt and ask that your love would help them to find healing and hope. We pray for all those who are unwell and ask that those around them would share your love today in a special way.
Lord, hear our prayer,

All   **Please.**

Voice 3   Green is the colour of life.
Dear God, we pray for those people who are working to bring love and life into places where there is war and injustice. We remember especially those in . . . and pray that men, women and children will have the courage to keep on working for peace and will discover love in unexpected places.
Lord, hear our prayer,

All   **Please.**

Voice 4   White is the colour of eternity.
Dear God, we give you thanks for your great love for every person. We pray that you would help your church to tell people of that love, and especially we pray for the church in . . .
We remember all the people we have loved but see no longer, and ask you to help us live lives of love for you and other people.
Lord, hear our prayer,

All   **Please.**

(*Voices hold all four colours together or hold a rainbow fabric/flag.*)

Voices   Dear God, thank you that the colours of the rainbow remind us of your promise to love us and to care for us. Be with us today and everyday.

All   **Amen.**

OR

If it is not possible to move around with the colours, simply use the colours to introduce each section of the prayers:

Voice 1   The colour yellow reminds us of joy, so let's give thanks and pray for those who bring us joy. (Use words above or similar.)

Voice 2   The colour red reminds us of pain and anger, so let's pray for all those who are struggling today. (Use words above or similar.)

Voice 3   The colour green reminds us of life and growth, so let's pray for those who work to bring about new beginnings. (Use words above or similar.)

Voice 4   The colour white reminds us of perfection and purity, so let's pray for the life of the church. (Use words above or similar.)

End prayers as above.

If this is a service of the word, then it may be appropriate to end the prayers with the Lord's Prayer before sharing the peace together.

If this is a Eucharist, continue with the peace, then the offertory and eucharistic prayers according to usual practice. You may like to invite people to pick up an unbroken heart as they return from receiving as a symbol of God's love for each person.

The peace

Introduce the peace, using these or similar words:

Minister   God makes peace within us – let us claim it.
God makes peace between us – let us share it.
The peace of the Lord be with you.

All   **And also with you.**[4]

➡ WE GO OUT

It may be appropriate to have notices at this point.

Hold up a basket of heart-shaped sweets (Love Hearts would be fun!).

Invite people to come forward, holding out both palms. Place one in the left hand with these or similar words: 'Because you are loved and lovely.'

Place a second into the right hand with these or similar words: 'Now pass it on and share love.'

Blessing

Minister   May the love of God be in your heart,
may the love of God be in our world,
and the blessing of God, Father, Son and Spirit,
be with you and all whom you love,
this day and always.
Amen.

Notes

1 *New Patterns for Worship*, London: Church House Publishing, 2008, p. 84, B40.
2 *New Patterns for Worship*, p. 95, B73. Copyright © Stuart Thomas and reproduced by kind permission.
3 *New Patterns for Worship*, p. 166, E12.
4 *New Women Included*, London: SPCK, 1996, p. 55.

A journey for everyone

This outline uses as its key texts the story of Jesus' temptations and the classic Ash Wednesday readings as a starting point. The journey is that made by Jesus out into the wilderness but also the journey we make through the weeks of Lent. During this time Christians explore the traditional disciplines of giving, fasting and prayer. This outline suggests that the whole church take on these disciplines in Lent.

The outline could be used on Sunday or mid week, in church or elsewhere.

Key lectionary readings

See note in Chapter 6, How to use the service outlines. If using this outline for a Church of England principal Sunday service in Lent, the lectionary readings must be those for the day.

Isaiah 58.1–12 'Real fasting'

Psalm 51.1–12 'Being really sorry'

Philippians 4.4–9 'Living well'

Luke 4.1–13 'Tempted in every way' AND Matthew 6.1–7, 16–18 'A way of life'

You will need

- Some pilgrim clothes
- Items to create prayer places: picnic blanket, basket, food, etc.; a poster montage of celebrities, a bowl of star-shaped confetti; large map of the world, heart shapes
- If you are unable to create prayer places (see p. 58), a bowl of sweets

WE GATHER

Opening hymn

Create a small procession made of 'pilgrims', wearing rough clothing, walking sticks, barefoot or sandals, rough backpack or satchel. If you usually have an altar procession, dress them in this way and process as usual. If you are not used to processions, invite a mixed-age group of around six people to take part. Walk in single file during the hymn.

When the procession reaches the front, the group kneel in various places around the front.

Informal welcome

Formal introduction

Minister	The Lord be with you.
All	**And also with you.**
Voice	Today is another day on our journey. We have decided to journey with Jesus, pilgrims through life. It's not always easy, but God is with us. Will you join us in the journey?
All	**We will.**
Voice	Please kneel. *(Everyone, including ministers, kneels.)*
Minister	Let's be still and remember God's presence with us.
	(After a 30-second pause:)
Voice	Will you join us in the journey?
All	**We will.**
Voice	Please stand. *(Everyone stands.)*
Voice	God is with us now.
All	**God is with us now.**

We say sorry

Making connections

Minister   It is the season of Lent, when we concentrate on what it means to follow Jesus. We know that we sometimes forget about him and sometimes ignore what we should do.

Pilgrim group   Create in me a clean heart, O God.

All   **Create in me a clean heart, O God.**

(Everyone looks down at the floor.)

For all the times we have forgotten to follow Jesus,
Lord, have mercy.

All   **Lord, have mercy.**

(Everyone turns to face the back of the church.)

For all the times we have turned our backs
on God,
Christ, have mercy,

All   **Christ, have mercy.**

(All turn to have backs to the outside walls)

For all the times we have turned our backs on
the people around us,
Lord, have mercy.

All   **Lord, have mercy.**

Pilgrim group   Create in me a clean heart, O God.

All   **Create in me a clean heart, O God.**

Minister   May almighty God,
who sent his Son into the world to save
   sinners,
bring *you* his pardon and peace, now and
   for ever.

All   **Amen.**[1]

Hymn

Collect or prayer for the day

See note in Chapter 6, How to use the service outlines.

Minister   Heavenly Father,
your Son battled with the powers of darkness,
and grew closer to you in the desert:
help us to use these days to grow in wisdom
   and prayer
that we may witness to your saving love
In Jesus Christ our Lord.
Amen.[2]

 WE LISTEN

Reading(s)

If you are using more than one reading, then read Isaiah and/or Philippians from a contemporary version.

Read the temptations Gospel (Luke) in the usual way.

Then introduce the talk with the following presentation, each reading is to be read from a different place in church, but the mime should happen at the front.

Reader 1   Luke 4.2–4 *(One person mimes blowing a trumpet and struts about looking important. Then stops and looks at each hand in turn, before putting hands behind back.)*

Reader 2   Luke 4.5–7 *(One person mimes looking very important, hands high, beckoning everyone to look at him or her. Then sits down and mimes closing a door.)*

Reader 3   Luke 4.16–18 *(One person mimes looking very miserable and makes streaks across his or her face. Then mimes smiling and nodding, combing hair.)*

Talk

Choose three of the pilgrims to stand at the front.

Ask people about their favourite meals. Draw out ideas of abundance and feasting.

Talk about how much food we waste in our world and how we always have enough. Our supermarkets are never empty! Say something similar to:

The first temptation Jesus faced was about food. Jesus was hungry – he could create food for himself and everyone else around. It seems like a good thing . . . but the little whisper underneath is: 'You can have whatever you want. You deserve it. You need a treat.' Anyone who has ever been on a diet will recognize these thoughts. Anyone who has ever had a bad day at school or office. Then we start surrounding ourselves with so much stuff that we can't see the important things any more – like God and other people's needs.

(Pilgrim 1 steps forward.)

Jesus asked us to fast. Fasting means to go without. Choose something to go without this Lent and every time you want that thing, think instead about God and God's world.

Ask people to name someone really, really successful or famous – a celebrity. Ask them to imagine what it feels like for everybody to look at them and tell them how fabulous they are; for people around them to do everything for them.

Talk about celebrities who have misused fame and fortune (there's always one in current headlines).

Jesus was tempted to take all the glory for himself, to do such amazing things that people would have no choice but to adore him. But Jesus wants us to remember that everything we have comes from God the Creator and to give God thanks and praise.

(Pilgrim 2 steps forward.)

Jesus asked us to pray, quietly, privately, daily. Prayer means turning away from our own ideas and listening to God. This Lent think about praying every day and praising God for everything he has done.

Ask people what they would do if they had a million pounds. Talk about game show/lottery winners and how they sometimes want things for themselves, sometimes for their families. Occasionally people want to do something spectacular and spend it all in a dramatic way.

The third temptation Jesus faced was to do something amazing, and risky! It would be fine because God would take care of what happened. It was about Jesus looking good and treating God lightly.

(Pilgrim 3 steps forward.)

Jesus asked us to give money to help other people, not to do anything as a trick or a stunt, but quietly and regularly give to other people. As we do this we place our trust in God, that he will take our small things and make a big difference in the lives of other people. In Lent we need to think about our money and give purposefully as we make the journey.

Three temptations, three actions, three pilgrims. But each of us can make this choice as we journey through Lent. We don't need to think about the stuff we need, we don't need to think about whether everyone will admire us or even about how we can make a really big gesture. The journey is about being who we are, and doing some ordinary

things faithfully every day: fasting, praying and giving. It's a journey for everyone.

The older ones can help the little ones, the little ones can encourage the older ones.

Encourage people to keep going.

NB: Children and fasting – there is not a problem with encouraging children to go without something. Muslim children fast regularly from the age of 7 during Ramadan, sometimes younger. But be mindful of those who may have eating problems.

WE RESPOND

Creed or statement of faith

Making connections

Minister We've thought about being on a journey together, encouraging each other as we follow Jesus. Let's remind ourselves of the things we believe as we say:

All **We believe in God the Father,
from whom every family
in heaven and on earth is named.**

**We believe in God the Son,
who lives in our hearts through faith,
and fills us with his love.**

**We believe in God the Holy Spirit,
who strengthens us
with power from on high.**

**We believe in one God,
Father, Son and Holy Spirit.
Amen.**[3]

Prayers

Create three prayer places in the church. They will need to be easily accessible.

Divide congregation into six pilgrim groups and send them to journey round the station prayer places together.

Prayer place 1

Place a picnic blanket on the floor or on a table. Put a basket on it with good-quality china, glasses, etc.

Put some bread, cheese, wine, cake, etc. out. Make it look abundant. Place some small pictures of other food and important items nearby – include items such as TV and computer (with Facebook showing if possible). On two cards (one for each group) have the following instructions:

Take a moment to think about all the food, and pick up one of the smaller pictures. Hold it quietly and think about going without. Ask God to help you to fast in Lent.

One person prays: Lord God, forgive us for being greedy. Help us to make good choices on our journey through Lent. Be with those who are hungry today and give courage and wisdom to those who want to make things better in our world. Amen.

Prayer place 2

Display a poster montage of celebrities and headlines about fame.

On a small table nearby place a bowl of star-shaped confetti, and a wooden cross on some gold fabric.

On two cards have the following instructions:

Pick up a handful of star confetti. Think for a moment about how wonderful God is and choose a word or two to describe God. Scatter your confetti over the cross, speaking aloud the words of praise you have chosen.

One person prays: Lord God, thank you for all the skills and gifts you give to us. We pray for all those people who teach us and encourage us to use our gifts to help others and give you glory. Help us to encourage each other on our journey with you. Amen.

Prayer place 3

Place a large map of the world on the floor or wall (preschool suppliers e.g. Early Learning Centre sell vinyl floor maps). Place a pile of heart shapes (post-it notes or paper).

On two cards have the following instructions:

As a group talk for a moment about places and situations where there is great need in the world or in our country. Give each person a heart, and invite everyone to place their forefingers firmly in the centre as they think about one situation they would like to change. Then place it on the map.

One person prays: Lord God, you know all the needs of the world. Be close to those who are struggling today, and help us to be generous with our time, money and

skills to make a difference. We pray especially for the work of (*add any organizations you are helping as a church*) . . . Amen.

When everyone has finished and returned to their seats, one person prays in these or similar words:

Lord God, we pray for the needs of our world and our community. As we go about our journeys each day, in our homes, our schools, our towns and our work, help us to share your love. Give strength and courage to all who are leading us on our journey and inspire all those who work for peace and justice. Amen.

OR

If you are not able to create prayer places or if your congregation would be unable to move around, then use the following idea.

(A person (perhaps one of the pilgrims) walks around with a bowl of sweets or grapes and invites everyone to take one – and eat it!)

Voice Lord God, your world is full of good things that we enjoy. We pray for all those who work on farms and in factories to bring us the things we like. We remember those who are anxious about providing enough for those they love, and we ask that you would help us through this Lent to make good choices about how we use our resources.
Lord, in your mercy
Hear our prayer.

(A person walks around with a bowl of star shapes and invites everyone to hold one.)

Voice Lord God, there are many people in our world who have responsibility, influence and power. We pray for all those in leadership that they will always work for the good of others and not for their own fame. We pray for those who work in media and entertainment, that they may find real fulfilment. We ask that you would help us through this Lent to turn towards you in prayer each day.
Lord, in your mercy
Hear our prayer.

(A person walks around with a bowl of chocolate coins or toy money (or small change!) and invites everyone to take a coin – and hold it.)

Voice Lord God, we have so many good things yet there is so much need in the world. We pray for all those organizations who are seeking to make a difference to others, and ask that you would give them wisdom and creativity in their work.

We remember also those whose needs cannot easily be met by money, especially those who are unwell or grieving . . . We ask that you would help us to be generous during this Lent as we make sacrifices on our journey of faith.
Lord, in your mercy
Hear our prayer.

If the service is a service of the word, it may be appropriate to end the prayers with the Lord's Prayer, before sharing the peace together. If the service is a Eucharist, continue with the peace followed by the bringing of gifts, the preparing of the table and the eucharistic prayer. Involve different generations as appropriate.

The peace

Introduce the peace, using these or similar words:

Minister   Christ is our peace.
He has reconciled us to God
in one body by the cross.
We meet in his name and share his peace.[4]
The peace of the Lord be with you.

All   And also with you.

 WE GO OUT

Notices may be included at this point as part of moving the focus to our Christian lives.

If you are using Lent to focus on a particular activity or charity there may be resources to give out as people leave.

Invite the pilgrims to lead people to gather around the door.

Then one of them prays:

Lord God, be with us as we journey on together through Lent.

(*Invite everyone to hold hands.*) Help us support one another.

(*Invite everyone to raise hands upwards.*) Help us to look to you each day.

(*Invite everyone to point forward.*) Help us to love the world.

Blessing

Minister   The love of the Lord Jesus
draw *you* to himself,
the power of the Lord Jesus
strengthen *you* in his service,
the joy of the Lord Jesus fill *your* hearts;
and the blessing . . .

All   Amen.[5]

Notes

1 *New Patterns for Worship*, London: Church House Publishing, 2008, p. 95, B71.
2 *Common Worship: Additional Collects*, London: Church House Publishing, 2004, p. 12.
3 *New Patterns for Worship*, p. 166, E12.
4 *New Patterns for Worship*, p. 274, H21.
5 *New Patterns for Worship*, p. 302, J63.

New life for everyone

In the companion volume to this book, *Festivals Together*, there are some special outlines for use at the various Easter festivals. This outline is to be used on a Sunday immediately following Easter and picks up on Easter themes. The activities and ideas are reflective and would work well with a smaller congregation.

Key lectionary readings

Please see note in Chapter 6, How to use the service outlines. Easter is a season that requires the set lectionary readings for the day in a Church of England principal service.

Psalm 16.5–11 'It's a good place to be'

1 John 4.7–15 'This is love'

Luke 24.36–44 'Living with the consequences'

You will need

- Pictures of: car, baby seat, bed, crib, meal, baby bottle, someone walking, pram/pushchair; smiley face
- A megaphone (or picture of one)
- A calendar or clock
- Small chocolate eggs or similar to give away

 ## WE GATHER

Opening hymn

Informal welcome

Formal introduction

Minister   Alleluia! Christ is risen!

All   **He is risen indeed! Alleluia!**[1]

Split the congregation into three. Invite one group to shout: 'Alleluia!!', the second group: 'Christ is risen!' and the third: 'He is risen indeed!' Repeat several times with enthusiasm.

Opening prayer

Voice   This is the day that the Lord has made. We will rejoice and be glad in it.
Inspire us in our worship, stretch us in our thinking, and change us in our lives.
Amen.

We say sorry

Making connections

Most churches will have a large cross somewhere during the season of Easter. Invite the congregation to gather around the cross, which might mean going outside.

Minister   Sometimes we are so glad that Jesus is alive we want to keep the news to ourselves. We forget to tell others and we forget to live as Good News people. The cross is empty now. The tomb is empty now for Jesus has risen from the dead. In this is love, not that we love God, but that he loved us and sent Jesus to be the atoning sacrifice for our sins.

Invite people to come forward and place a hand on the cross, and pause for a moment thanking God for his forgiveness and grace.

When everyone has done this:

Minister   We are often slow to follow the example of Christ.
Lord, have mercy.

All   **Lord, have mercy.**

Minister	We often fail to be known as Christ's disciples. Christ, have mercy.
All	**Christ, have mercy.**
Minister	We often fail to walk the way of the cross. Lord, have mercy.
All	**Lord, have mercy.**[2]
Minister	May almighty God, who sent his Son into the world to save sinners, bring *you* his pardon and peace, now and for ever.
All	**Amen.**[3]

If you are outside or some distance from the seats, use the next hymn as a processional to return.

Hymn/Gloria

Collect or prayer for the day

See note in Chapter 6, How to use the service outlines.

Minister	Risen Christ, who calls us to walk in love, touch our lives with hope, give us courage to believe and fill us with joy at the good news that you have overcome death and opened for us the way to eternal life. Amen.

 WE LISTEN

Reading(s)

If numbers permit, gather everyone together into a story space.

Use someone who is good at storytelling to create an atmosphere of tension and fear. Then tell the story.

Use *The Book of Books* by Trevor Dennis[4] or another story version of the reading.

At the end say: 'This is the gospel of the Lord' three times, getting louder and standing for the last shout.

Talk

Keep everyone gathered together and talk about times of good news. Invite older people to reminisce about when they got engaged or the birth of a baby. Children might remember a new baby arriving or an announcement about moving house. Say something similar to:

When we hear good news we feel really glad at first. But when something really, really big happens, it takes a long time to get used to it.
Think about what has to happen after a baby is born.

(*Show picture of car.*) Can't just drive away – need a baby seat (*show picture*).

(*Show picture of bed.*) Can't just put baby to sleep – need a cot (*show picture*).

(*Show picture of mealtime.*) Can't just share your food – need milk (*show picture of a baby bottle*).

(*Show picture of someone walking.*) Can't just pop into the shops – need a pram/pushchair (*show picture*).

So much has to change.

Invite people to share ideas/memories about how life changed: it takes time to get used to and it requires us to do things differently.

Ask them to imagine what it was like when people first heard about Jesus coming back from the dead.

First there was the excitement and 'I can't believe it' or 'I don't believe it' moments. Then there was a fear of what might happen next. But Jesus came and did ordinary things with them. He did something familiar – ate a meal with them. Then he began to explain how things would be different for them. (*Show a Bible.*)

All the things that used to seem so difficult to understand – Jesus explained them. (*Hold up a smiley face.*)

(*Show a megaphone (or picture of one).*) They can't just sit around remembering. Jesus tells them to go and tell everyone the good news. He told them to tell people the good news that God forgives sins. (*Hold up a smiley face.*)

(*Show picture of calendar/clock.*) They can't rush about aimlessly. Jesus tells them to wait for God's Holy Spirit to come with power. (*Hold up a smiley face.*)

The good news about Jesus takes time to sink in. And it will change our lives for ever.

 **WE RESPOND**

Creed or statement of faith

Making connections

Minister	We've thought about how the good news of Jesus' new life changes our lives. Let's remind ourselves of the things we believe as we say:
All	**Christ died for our sins** **in accordance with the Scriptures;** **he was buried;** **he was raised to life on the third day** **in accordance with the Scriptures;** **afterwards he appeared to his followers,** **and to all the apostles:** **this we have received,** **and this we believe.** **Amen.**[5]

Prayers

Voice	Lord, hear our prayer,
All	**Please.**
	(Invite people to hold out both hands with just thumbs visible.)
Voice	Lord Jesus, your new life is good news for the whole world. We pray especially for those who help us to understand what the good news means. Help the Church here and everywhere to be bold in telling people about new life in Jesus. Lord, hear our prayer,
All	**Please.**
	(Invite people to hold out both hands, open palms.)
Voice	Lord Jesus, your new life is good news to all nations. We pray for those places where there is little joy or peace, especially remembering . . . Help those men, women and children who work for change and give them hope. Lord, hear our prayer,
All	**Please.**
	(Invite people to lay one hand on top of the other.)
Voice	Lord Jesus, your new life is good news to the people we know. We pray for the places where we live and the places where we go each day. We remember those who specially need to hear good news today, particularly . . . Help all of us to share your love with those we meet. Lord, hear our prayer,

All	**Please.**
	(Invite people to clasp hands together.)
Voice	Lord Jesus, your new life is good news for me. Help me to be confident in telling other people, to wait for your power in my life and to understand your word as I follow you each day. Lord, hear our prayer,
All	**Please.**

If the service is a service of the word, it may be appropriate to end the prayers with the Lord's Prayer, before sharing the peace together. If the service is a Eucharist, continue with the peace followed by the bringing of gifts, the preparing of the table and the eucharistic prayer. Involve different generations as appropriate.

The peace

Introduce the peace, using these or similar words:

Minister	The risen Christ came and stood among his disciples and said, 'Peace be with you.' Then were they glad when they saw the Lord. Alleluia.[6] The peace of the Lord be with you.
All	**And also with you.**

 **WE GO OUT**

Notices may be included at this point as part of moving the focus to our Christian lives.

Invite people to take a small token of good news to share with someone else (a chocolate egg or flower might be appropriate).

Remind people that Easter is a season – so it is a surprise to neighbours and friends that we are still celebrating.

Voice	The Father has sent his Son as the Saviour of the world.
Voice	Forgiveness of sins is to be proclaimed in his name.
Voice	Go in peace and love to share the news. Alleluia!
All	**In the name of Christ. Alleluia!**

Blessing

Minister   May Christ,
who out of defeat brings new hope and a new
    future,
fill you with his new life;
and the blessing of the Father, the Son and the
    Holy Spirit
be with you this day and always.
Amen.[7]

Notes

1 *New Patterns for Worship*, London: Church House Publishing, 2008, p. 68, A31.
2 *New Patterns for Worship*, p. 92, B58.
3 *New Patterns for Worship*, p. 95, B71.
4 Trevor Dennis, *The Book of Books*, Oxford: Lion Hudson, 2009, p. 400.
5 *New Patterns for Worship*, p. 165, E10.
6 *New Patterns for Worship*, p. 274, H22.
7 *New Patterns for Worship*, p. 308, J85.

May

A place for everyone

Whether Easter falls early or late, the month of May will include readings from the book of Acts. The story of the early Church is read alongside some of the letters written by Peter and John, and the Gospel readings for this season include many of the images that Jesus spoke of and acted out to explore the life of discipleship. Over and over again it becomes clear that as Christians come together there will be a place for everyone.

This worship outline can be used at any time during May and although it highlights some of the lectionary readings, the worship, prayer and teaching could be used with the weekly lectionary as appropriate.

Key lectionary readings

Please see note in Chapter 6, How to use the service outlines.

1 Peter 2.2–10 'Living stones'

Acts 8.26–40 ' It could be you'

John 10.1–10 'The good shepherd'

You will need

- A basket containing
  - a variety of flower petals
  - leaves
  - shells, etc.
- A magnet

 WE GATHER

Opening hymn

Informal welcome

Formal introduction

Minister	Alleluia! Christ is risen!
All	**He is risen indeed! Alleluia!**[1]
	(*Voice(s) come from different parts of the church:*)
Voice	Come on, everyone, praise the Lord!
All	**Come on, everyone, praise the Lord!**
Voice	Who is everyone?
All	**Who is everyone?**
Voice	I am! (*Points to self.*)
All	**I am!** (*Everyone points to himself or herself.*)
Voice	You are! (*Points to someone else.*)
All	**You are!** (*Each person points to someone else.*)
Voice	Who is everyone?
All	**Who is everyone?**
Voice	We are! (*Join hands with neighbour and raise high.*)
All	**We are!** (*Join hands with neighbours and raise high.*)
Voice	Come on, everyone, praise the Lord!
All	**Come on, everyone, praise the Lord!**

We say sorry

Making connections

Minister	As we remember that there is room for everyone in God's house, we also remember those times when we have forgotten to include others, whether on purpose or by accident.

We remember those times when we have not made room for God's love in our lives and those times when our world seems full of anger and hate.

Pass a basket of varied flower petals/leaves/shells, etc. around the congregation and invite each person to take one thing from the basket and hold it. In a large congregation you may need more than one basket. Play music while this is happening.

When everyone is holding an object:

Voice	Forgive us for forgetting that each and every person is special to you. Forgive us for not listening or welcoming others. Lord, have mercy.
All	**Lord, have mercy.**
Voice	forgive us for the times that we have neglected or hurt others. Forgive us for not speaking out for those who no one hears Christ, have mercy.
All	**Christ, have mercy.**
Voice	Forgive us for forgetting that you love each one of us. Forgive us for not living each day as those who are loved by you. Lord, have mercy.
All	**Lord, have mercy.**
Minister	May the God of love bring *us* back to himself, forgive *us our* sins, and assure *us* of his eternal love in Jesus Christ our Lord.
All	**Amen.**[2]

Hymn/Gloria

Collect or prayer for the day

See note in Chapter 6, How to use the service outlines.

Minister	God of welcome, who calls each one of us to follow, give us the faith to know that we belong, give us the vision to open our doors and build your church, so that your love might shine out in this and every place; through Jesus Christ our risen Lord, Amen.

WE LISTEN

Reading(s)

The key reading is the reading from Acts which can be read as a moving drama. See Additional resource: May on p. 68 for script.

Talk

Begin with a person simply wandering across the front of church and going over to a window or object of interest (e.g. an old tomb). After a few minutes this person beckons to the congregation, indicating that others should come and look (you may want to prime a few in case people are slow to start). One or two also start peering and looking, then beckon a few more. Keep going until most people are going to have a look!

Ask people if they have ever seen a crowd gathering and gone to find out what is happening. It might be a sales demonstration in the mall, or an unexpected piece of street theatre – perhaps people have been to Covent Garden or the Edinburgh festival where comedians, magicians, dancers and singers draw crowds. These kinds of crowds only last for as long as the act, but there are other kinds of crowds, like those going to watch a sporting event or to see a band they really like. Then everyone has something in common – whether people are rich or poor, young or old no longer matters, all are being drawn to the event. Say something similar to:

> Jesus often talked about gathering people around him. He was a kind of magnet – attracting all kinds of people to listen and follow him. He never turned people away. He talked of himself as a shepherd or a light or a vine – and shepherds, vines and lights all have other things around them.

Ask people if they know how a magnet works – maybe have one to demonstrate.

> The things that stick to a magnet become magnetized: they become magnets too!

> The people who gathered around Jesus went off to tell other people his story. They discovered that wherever they went people wanted to hear more – and it wasn't just people they knew and liked. Philip

discovered that a person from very far away – an Ethiopian – wanted to hear. They were drawn together as if by a magnet!

The people who gathered around Jesus prayed together and worshipped together; they went to tell others, to baptize and to teach: all things that happen over and over again in the book of Acts as the good news about Jesus spreads. There is a place for everyone!

 ## WE RESPOND

Creed or statement of faith

Making connections

Minister We've thought about how the good news of Jesus' new life changes our lives. Let's remind ourselves of the things we believe: as we say:

All **We believe in God the Father,**
from whom every family
in heaven and on earth is named.

We believe in God the Son,
who lives in our hearts through faith,
and fills us with his love.

We believe in God the Holy Spirit,
who strengthens us
with power from on high.

We believe in one God,
Father, Son and Holy Spirit.
Amen.[3]

Prayers

These prayers could be done in small groups or led from the front.

Voice Lord, hear our prayer,

All **Please.**

(Invite people to stand in small groups.)

Voice Lord God, we pray for your Church throughout the world as people gather to pray and to praise. Give courage to those who face difficulties; give wisdom to those who lead; and give us all a heart to welcome others into our midst.
Lord, hear our prayer,

All **Please.**

(Invite people to kneel if possible, or clasp hands in prayer.)

Voice Lord God, you have called us to be people who gather around you, who read your word, listen to your voice, and share the concerns of our lives in prayer. Inspire those who teach us how to pray and strengthen all of us so that we can learn more about praying together.
Lord, hear our prayer,

All **Please.**

(Invite people to stand up and look towards the doors.)

Voice Lord God, you have called us to be people who tell others the good news about Jesus. Give us confidence to speak about all that you have done. We pray especially for the things we are doing in our community, particularly when we reach out to those people who feel neglected and unloved.
Lord, hear our prayer,

All **Please.**

(Invite people to put a hand on someone's shoulder.)

Voice Lord God, you have called us to be people who help others. We pray for those who help their friends, colleagues and neighbours and we pray for those who are working for peace and justice in our world. Give us love and compassion for those in need, give us ears to listen and eyes to see the needs around us, and give us the vision to take action where help is needed.
Lord, hear our prayer,

All **Please.**

(Invite people to hold hands and make a star with others nearby. Those who are bold can circle slowly during this prayer!)

Voice Lord God, you have called us to life in all its fullness. Help us to be faithful in following you day by day. Fill us with joy, give us words of welcome, and help us to dance with delight because of all that you have done.
Lord, hear our prayer,

All **Please.**

If the service is a service of the word, it may be appropriate to end the prayers with the Lord's Prayer, before sharing the peace together. If the service is a Eucharist, continue with the peace followed by the bringing of gifts, the preparing of the table and the eucharistic prayer. Involve different generations as appropriate.

The peace

Introduce the peace, using these or similar words:

Minister   God makes peace within us – let us claim it.
God makes peace between us – let us share it.
The peace of the Lord be with you.

All   **And also with you.**[4]

 ## WE GO OUT

Notices may be included at this point as part of moving the focus to our Christian lives.

Invite everyone to turn and face the door which should be flung open. Someone could ring a bell (like a town crier).

Voices   Listen, everyone! There's a place for everyone with God's people.

As we go out we pray that people will come in.
As we come in we pray that we will bring others with us.
As we go out and as we come in, Jesus is with us!
Go in peace to love and serve the Lord.
Thanks be to God!

Blessing

Minister   May the peace of Jesus be in your hearts;
may the joy of Jesus be on your lips;
may the hope of Jesus be in your life;
and the blessing of God . . .

Notes

1 *New Patterns for Worship*, London: Church House Publishing, 2008, p. 68, A31.
2 *New Patterns for Worship*, p. 95, B73. Copyright © Stuart Thomas and reproduced by kind permission.
3 *New Patterns for Worship*, p. 166, E12.
4 *New Women Included*, London: SPCK, 1996, p. 55.

Philip and the Ethiopian (Acts 8.26–40)

You will need two people, Philip and the Ethiopian, starting from different places in the church, far away from each other; plus a commentator, and an angel voice.

Commentator (standing high up somewhere)   It's amazing from up here. I have a bird's eye view of the whole scene. Over on my left is Philip, wandering around, chatting to his friends, talking (again) about Jesus.

Over on my right far, far away is a man in a chariot. He comes from Ethiopia. (*Squints a bit*) I can tell by what he is wearing that he is pretty important. Yes, I think he works for the Candace, queen of all Ethiopia. He doesn't just work for her, oh no. He is in charge of her whole treasury. A pretty clever chap, I think. He's been to Jerusalem to worship and now he's going home.

Watch him as he journeys in his chariot.

(*Ethiopian moves towards the front, reading a book.*)

Oh, and now look, over to my left, something is happening. Philip has seen something, Or maybe he's heard something . . . Yes . . . It's . . . it's, it's an angel! An angel is talking to Philip!

Angel voice   Get up, Philip, get up and move! Move yourself down south to the road that goes from Jerusalem to Gaza.

Commentator   Wouldn't fancy that myself. It's a bit of a way-out place and a bit of a journey.

(*Philip starts to walk towards the area where the Ethiopian is travelling.*)

Angel voice   Get over to that chariot, Philip, get going and get talking!

Commentator   Wow! How did that happen? Philip is right next to the chariot!!

(*Philip is now walking by the side of the Ethiopian.*)

Philip   Is that a good book, mate? Do you know what it's about?

Ethiopian   This? How can I understand it unless someone gives me a bit of help?

Commentator   Oh my goodness! Philip is getting in the chariot. He is talking to the Ethiopian. Yes, yes, I can see, they are chatting away together.

(*Voice reads verses 32 and 33.*)

Ethiopian   So, my friend, can you tell me what this bit is about? Is it about someone in particular?

Commentator   And yes, Philip is telling him about Jesus . . . it's amazing! Oh, and they are coming up to some water now. Will the chariot go through it or round it? Will the horses stop for a drink? Will Philip stop for a drink?

Ethiopian   Look! We are by some water. I could get baptized! What's to stop me?

Commentator   Didn't see that coming! But the chariot has stopped and Philip is indeed baptizing the Ethiopian. That is a surprise! (*Philip needs to hide and slip away.*) Oh . . . and now Philip has gone! Where's he gone? The Ethiopian is on his own again . . . Where's Philip? (*Commentator strains his eyes looking round the church.*) Oh, I see now. He's way over there telling everyone the good news about Jesus!

June

Choices for everyone

As we move into Ordinary Time, the lectionary encourages us to think about what it means to be a disciple. The readings face us with the consequences of our decisions, whether in the Old Testament through the keeping of commandments and the desire to know God, or through the letters of encouragement written by Paul and others to help the early Christians understand what Jesus' life and death really meant. The Gospel readings introduce us to people who had to decide just what Jesus meant for them and to them, as well as exploring what it means to choose to follow Jesus.

Key lectionary readings

Please see note in Chapter 6, How to use the service outlines.

Deuteronomy 11.18–28 'The whole of life'

2 Corinthians 4.5–12 'Living for Jesus'

Luke 7.36—8.3 'Choosing to go public'

You will need

- Items for four prayer stations:
  - a globe or map of the world, pictures and headlines of current events
  - large photo or map of your community, coloured blocks
  - symbols to represent your church
  - a mirror
  - photos of people
- Papers cut to represent voting slips
- Cards prepared with words on as indicated

 WE GATHER

Opening hymn

Informal welcome

Minister   Today we are thinking about choices: the choice to follow Jesus; the choice to worship him; the choice to live the way he wants us to. Let's choose now to praise his name.

Praise shout

This can be done like a US army-style marching song.

Voice	Come on, everyone, praise the Lord!
All	**Come on, everyone, praise the Lord!**
Voice	He's the one to be adored.
All	**He's the one to be adored.**
Voice	Praise him! He's the best!
All	**Praise Him! He's the best!**
Voice	Praise Him! Forget the rest!
All	**Praise Him! Forget the rest!**

We say sorry

Making connections

Minister   Sometimes we make good choices, but there are times when we make wrong choices. Sometimes we do and say things that hurt others and hurt God's world. Sometimes we choose to do nothing instead of taking action. Sometimes we choose to turn away from God.

Let's be still and ask God to come close to us as we say sorry for all our wrong choices.

(Turn out all the lights.)

Voice   I will say 'Let the darkness cover me, and the night wrap itself around me. Even darkness

is not dark to you, and night is as clear as
the day.'

(Be still in the darkness for a minute. Then all say:)

All   **Lord, have mercy/Christ, have mercy/Lord,
have mercy.**

(Turn lights back on.)

Minister   May the God of love and power
forgive *you* and free *you* from *your* sins,
heal and strengthen *you* by his Spirit,
and raise *you* to new life in Christ our Lord.

All   **Amen.**[1]

Hymn/Gloria

Collect or prayer for the day

See note in Chapter 6, How to use the service outlines.

Minister   God of wisdom,
source of all knowledge,
who promises to be with us always,
send your Holy Spirit
to lead us into all truth
and to give us understanding;
in the name of Jesus, your Son
Amen.

 ## WE LISTEN

Reading(s)

Use story version of the Bible for the Gospel reading.

Talk

Invite those who wish to join in with the Choice
game.

Read a statement and they simply have to
choose the answer – true or false.

If space permits, this can be done by moving to
two different points in the building.

Five or six statements will be enough, e.g.

- Chocolate has more calories than lettuce. (True)
- Football has more participants than fishing.
  (False)
- Wales has more people than Scotland. (False)

These should be funny and guessable rather
than based on knowledge so all ages can join in.

When game is over, everyone sits down.

Talk about the choices already made today –
e.g. coming to church, what to have for
breakfast. What about things we don't even
think about? Ask for suggestions. There are little
choices and big choices, and some of them
have surprising consequences. Say something
similar to:

Many of those who met or heard of Jesus faced a
choice: the choice was whether to do something or
to do nothing, to go and speak to Jesus or go home
again. In the story the woman chose to go public
with her love for Jesus. By pouring perfumed
ointment on his feet she was showing that she
thought he was a very special person. It was as if
she was worshipping him – and only God is worthy
of worship! I wonder what the consequences might
have been for her . . . or for any of those present
that day?

It's not always easy to make choices – that's why
books and films love playing with the big 'what if'
question: what if I do this or what if I don't? The
film *Sliding Doors* plays with this idea. Other films
make us think: remember the end of *ET* – would
ET stay or go? (He went back to his home.)
Sometimes choices are about doing good or not –
as when Edmund in *The Lion, the Witch and the
Wardrobe* chose to lie about having met the
White Queen.

All of us make little choices every day. Sometimes
those choices are bigger, like whether to take a
new job or saying hello to a new person at
school.

But the biggest choice we will make is the choice
about Jesus. Are we willing, like so many of those
who met him, to do or say things that reveal that
we believe that he is our Saviour? If we do then
there will be consequences!

 ## WE RESPOND

Creed or statement of faith

Making connections

Minister   We've thought about how the good news of
Jesus' new life changes our lives. Let's remind
ourselves of the things we believe:

Do you believe and trust in God the Father,
source of all being and life,
the one for whom we exist?

All	**We believe and trust in him.**
Minister	Do you believe and trust in God the Son, who took our human nature, died for us and rose again?
All	**We believe and trust in him.**
Minister	Do you believe and trust in God the Holy Spirit, who gives life to the people of God and makes Christ known in the world?
All	**We believe and trust in him.**
Minister	This is the faith of the Church.
All	**This is our faith.** **We believe and trust in one God, Father, Son and Holy Spirit. Amen.**[2]

Prayers

Set up four stations around the church. At each station there should be slips of paper and a 'ballot box'.

Station 1: the world

Put a globe or map of the world onto a table. Place pictures and headlines around about some of the things that are happening in our world.

Prepare a card that says:

> **Choose peace! Pray for those who are working for peace in the world, and those who are struggling in unjust situations.**
>
> **Pick up a voting slip and put it in the box as a sign of your choice to pray for these situations. If you want you can write a prayer on the paper.**

Station 2: the community

Place a map or large photo of your community on the floor. Put coloured blocks on the map to indicate places of significance, e.g. school, surgery, shops, playground. You might put other symbols to indicate important local issues.

Prepare a card that says:

> **Choose healing! Pray for those who come into our community to help others, and pray for those who are finding life difficult.**
>
> **Pick up a voting slip and put it in the box as a sign of your choice to pray for these situations. If you want you can write a prayer on the paper.**

Station 3: the church

Place some symbols that represent your church onto a small table. Include information about some of the things you are doing, such as a parish magazine, posters, baptism registers.

Prepare a card that says:

> **Choose good news! Pray for the life of the church, for the contacts with others outside, for those who lead and those who serve.**
>
> **Pick up a voting slip and place it in the box as a sign of your prayer. If you wish you can write a prayer on the paper.**

Station 4: ourselves

Prop a mirror against a wall, and place photos of people all around.

Prepare a card that says:

> **Choose life! Pray for yourself and those you love, that you may choose each day to follow Jesus and know life in all its fullness.**
>
> **Pick up a voting slip and place it in the box as a sign of your prayer. If you wish you can write a prayer on the paper.**

When everyone has visited all the stations, gather all the prayers together in these or similar words:

> Loving God, you listen to the things on our minds and in our hearts. You love the people we love. You care for the world more than we ever can. Accept our prayers today, for the sake of Jesus our Saviour. Amen.

OR

If you are unable to create stations around the church, invite four groups of people to create prayers using these or similar words. Instead of voting slips, invite people to raise a hand when they say the response to the prayers.

Minister	Loving God, we pray for your world and especially for men, women and children who are working for peace in difficult situations. We remember those who speak out against injustice, those who fear for the future and those who struggle to get through each day. Today we remember especially . . . Lord, hear our prayer,
All	**Please.** (*Raise hand.*)
Minister	Loving God, we pray for our community, especially remembering all those who come

here to work and to help. We remember doctors, community nurses, teachers, those who bring meals and many others, and we ask that you would give them compassionate hearts as they do their work. We pray too for those we know who are unwell or finding life difficult . . .
Lord, hear our prayer,

All **Please.** *(Raise hand.)*

Minister Loving God, we pray for our church, especially remembering all the different activities we are involved with. We pray for each of us as we talk to our neighbours, and we ask you to give wisdom to all those who lead and serve us.
Lord, hear our prayer,

All **Please.** *(Raise hand.)*

Minister Loving God, we pray for ourselves and for all those we love. Help us to choose each day to follow Jesus and to know life in all its fullness.
Lord, hear our prayer,

All **Please.** *(Raise hand.)*

Minister Loving God, you listen to the things on our hearts and minds. You love the people we love. You care for the world more than we ever can. Accept our prayers today, for the sake of Jesus our Saviour. Amen.

If the service is a service of the word, it may be appropriate to end the prayers with the Lord's Prayer, before sharing the peace together. If the service is a Eucharist, continue with the peace followed by the bringing of gifts, the preparing of the table and the eucharistic prayer. Involve different generations as appropriate.

The peace

Introduce the peace, using these or similar words:

Minister God makes peace within us – let us claim it.
God makes peace between us – let us share it.
The peace of the Lord be with you.

All **And also with you.**[3]

 # WE GO OUT

Notices may be included at this point as part of moving the focus to our Christian lives.

Invite people to make a simple gesture using thumb and forefinger as if holding a slip of paper and posting it. Practise a few times.

Then, as you make the gesture, say:

Jesus, we choose to follow you this day, this week and always. Amen.

Encourage people to make this gesture during the week ahead as they face choices each day.

Blessing

Minister May the God of grace guard your going out and your coming home,
keep you as you work and as you play,
as you think and as you act,
as you listen and as you talk
and hold you in the palm of his hand.
And the blessing of God, Father,
Son and Holy Spirit,
be with you all, this day and always,
Amen.

Notes

1 *New Patterns for Worship*, London: Church House Publishing, 2008, p. 97, B80.
2 *New Patterns for Worship*, p. 163, E6.
3 *New Women Included*, London: SPCK, 1996, p. 55.

Hope for everyone

This outline continues the theme of discipleship that the lectionary explores during Ordinary Time. The key focus for this month is that those who follow Jesus discover hope, which is sometimes experienced as physical healing, sometimes as a lifting of burdens, but once experienced is to be taken and shared with others. There is a real sense of being sent out into the world to take this message of hope to others.

Key lectionary readings

Please see note in Chapter 6, How to use the service outlines.

Isaiah 55.10–13 'The sure promise'

Ephesians 2.11–22 'He is our peace'

Luke 10.1–11, 16–20 'Carry nothing but hope'

You will need

- Enough pieces of paper (suggest A5) for everyone
- A large envelope labelled 'Secret Mission' containing one piece of paper as specified; large rucksack labelled 'Secret Mission Bag' containing rations, flask, maps, compass, spare underwear, set of detailed instructions, etc.
- Enough small envelopes for everyone enclosing a slip of paper with the references for the readings of the day

WE GATHER

Hand out sheets of paper to everyone as they arrive.

Opening hymn

Formal introduction

Minister   The Lord be with you.

All   **And also with you.**

Informal welcome

Minister   Today we are thinking about the hope that we have in Jesus, about a God who keeps his promises, and how we can take that message to those around us.

You will need to place several people around the edges of the worship/seating area.

Each of them is to be given a text which they begin to whisper, then speak more and more loudly. Each person keeps repeating the given phrase:

- 'Ho, everyone . . . come to the waters, come to the waters'
- 'Listen carefully to me, eat what is good'
- 'Listen so that you may live'
- 'Seek the Lord'
- 'Call upon him while he is near'

Finally:

All voices   (*shout*) Listen!

Single voice   For God is speaking today.

All   **Amen.**

We say sorry

Making connections

Minister	Sometimes we forget to be people of hope and healing. Sometimes we forget to follow God's ways, but he is faithful and has promised forgiveness. In the stillness we ask his forgiveness now for all that has gone wrong in our lives.
	(*Invite everyone to take the piece of paper they were given as they arrived and to tear it in half once.*)
Voice	Forgive us, Lord, for all the things we have done that harm other people and harm the world. Lord, have mercy.
All	**Lord, have mercy.**
	(*Invite everyone to tear the paper again.*)
Voice	Forgive us, Lord, for all the times we have ignored your promises to us and forgotten how to share your love. Christ, have mercy.
All	**Christ, have mercy.**
	(*Invite everyone to tear the paper again.*)
Voice	Forgive us Lord, for swapping hope for indifference when we see all that is wrong in our world and our lives. Lord, have mercy.
All	**Lord have mercy.**
	(*In silence collect up all the torn paper pieces, and simply place them in front of the Communion table.*)
Minister	May the God of love and power forgive *you* and free *you* from *your* sins, heal and strengthen *you* by his Spirit, and raise *you* to new life in Christ our Lord.
All	**Amen.**[1]

Hymn/Gloria

Collect or prayer for the day

See note in Chapter 6, How to use the service outlines.

Minister	God our Saviour, look on this wounded world in pity and in power; hold us fast to your promises of peace won for us by your Son, our Saviour Jesus Christ. Amen.[2]

WE LISTEN

Reading(s)

If you are using more than one reading, use contemporary versions.

Talk

Take out a large envelope with the words 'Secret Mission' written on it.

Talk about what kind of mission this might be. Ask people for ideas about how they might feel if asked to take on such a mission – excited, nervous, afraid?

What might they want to know? What might they want to take with them?

Show a large rucksack labelled 'Secret Mission Bag'. Pull out some things from the bag, e.g. food rations, flask, maps, spare underwear, compass, and a set of detailed instructions.

Hold up the envelope again and speculate about whether all this will be needed for the 'secret mission'.

Recap what a mission might be for – draw on some war-time stories if appropriate. Suggest that missions are sometimes undertaken to rescue people, to get information, to explore.

Open the envelope. Inside there should be one sheet of paper saying:

'Go and tell people God's kingdom is near. Speak peace.

'Take nothing with you – no money, no bag, no shoes.

From Jesus.'

Ask people what they think of these instructions. Think about how the instruction is very basic; say that we might want to know more – but the mission is simple. Point out that there is a message of hope, a message that can be depended on for God's kingdom is close, and when God speaks we know that things are going to happen. Say something similar to:

The disciples had learned to trust Jesus – they had watched him heal people, set them free, teach them new things, show them new ways of living. Now they were ready to do the same . . . and it worked.

Turn over the envelope again. Wonder who it might be for . . . then read out the names of some people in the congregation and/or the name of the church.

This is our mission. We are people of hope with a message of hope. The instructions remain the same. We don't need loads of special equipment, just ourselves, full of excitement because of all that Jesus does.

 WE RESPOND

Creed or statement of faith

Making connections

Minister We've thought about being on a journey together, encouraging each other as we follow Jesus. Let's remind ourselves of the things we believe as we say:

All   **We believe in God the Father,**
from whom every family
in heaven and on earth is named.

We believe in God the Son,
who lives in our hearts through faith,
and fills us with his love.

We believe in God the Holy Spirit,
who strengthens us
with power from on high.

We believe in one God,
Father, Son and Holy Spirit.
Amen.[3]

Prayers

Time travel

This prayer activity involves moving around the space. Those who are unable to move are encouraged to follow the journey in their imagination.

Invite everyone to move to the back of the church.

Voice   Look down at the ground beneath your feet. Imagine standing here when there was nothing but a meadow, a few sheep, some farm workers, the sound of a horse's hooves, or perhaps the sounds of a market, babies crying, women at the pump. All those centuries ago (*add age of your church building as appropriate*) someone came here to this place with a message of hope, a message of good news of God's love, and the people began to have hope and to plan for the future. They began to build this place. Lord God, thank you for those who brought the news here. We pray for all those who still work today to speak of your love and hope to our world. We pray for missionaries in . . . (*use church/diocese links*) and for those right here who share hope in our community.

(*Invite everyone to move towards the door, which should be opened.*)

Voice   Look round our building, then look outside the door. Think of all the changes that have happened, the alterations to the building, the wars, the plagues, the struggle against hard times. And through all of that God is faithful and God's people have spoken words of hope.

Lord God, we thank you for your faithfulness down the centuries. We continue to pray for peace in our world, and ask that you give courage to men, women and children of faith who continue to speak of hope and work for peace in difficult situations. We pray especially for . . . and ask for your healing and peace to come.

(*Invite everyone to move to the chancel area.*)

Voice   Look around at all the beautiful things in our church – the organ, the windows, the altar cloths, the flowers (*name as appropriate*). Each one of these things has a story to tell, a story of generosity and service, of people who trusted God and want to give him thanks and praise.

Lord God, we thank you for the people who serve this church, even today. We pray for those who lead worship, who speak, clean, serve and help. We pray for the work we do in the church and the work we do beyond. Help us to be people of hope in our daily lives and to share the good news of your love with those we meet. Especially we pray for those who need to know your hope today . . .

(*Invite everyone to look up at the roof.*)

Voice   Look up and think of the sky beyond the roof. Think of all the possibilities, of the things that are yet to happen, the future life of this place and the community round about.

We thank you, Lord, for calling us to follow
you and ask that you would help us to work
together so that your kingdom of love and hope
would be close to each of us and to those we
love . . .
(*Return to seats.*)

OR

If people can't move (either individually or because
space doesn't allow it) then invite people to turn to
look in the directions indicated.

If the service is a service of the word, it may be
appropriate to end the prayers with the Lord's
Prayer, before sharing the peace together. If the
service is a Eucharist, continue with the peace
followed by the bringing of gifts, the preparing
of the table and the eucharistic prayer. Involve
different generations as appropriate.

The peace

Introduce the peace, using these or similar words:

Minister   God makes peace within us – let us claim it.
God makes peace between us – let us share it.
The peace of the Lord be with you.

All   **And also with you.**[4]

 ## WE GO OUT

Notices may be included at this point as part of
moving the focus to our Christian lives.

Hand people an envelope as they leave with the words
'Your Mission' on the outside. Inside is a slip of paper
with the references from the readings of the day.

Blessing

Minister   The love of the Lord Jesus
draw *you* to himself,
the power of the Lord Jesus
strengthen *you* in his service,
the joy of the Lord Jesus fill *your* hearts;
and the blessing of God,
the Father, the Son and the Holy Spirit
be with you this day and always.
Amen.[5]

Notes

1 *New Patterns for Worship*, London: Church House Publishing,
2008, p. 97, B80.
2 *Common Worship: Additional Collects*, London: Church House
Publishing, 2004, p. 19.
3 *New Patterns for Worship*, p. 166, E12.
4 *New Women Included*, London: SPCK, 1996, p. 55.
5 *New Patterns for Worship*, p. 302, J63.

Jesus for everyone

This outline focuses on Jesus, and the question of identity which runs through the summer readings. This question is explored through miracles, including the feeding of the five thousand, and through teaching. It is reinforced in Old Testament prophecies and promises, and encouragement as to how to live in the light of Jesus comes through the Epistles. During August congregations often take on different shapes, with regulars absent and visitors present, and a more relaxed and informal feel.

Key lectionary readings

Please see note in Chapter 6, How to use the service outlines.

Isaiah 58.9–14 'Abundant living'

Romans 10.5–15 'Everyone who calls'

Matthew 14.13–21 'Food for thought'

You will need

- An African drum (not essential)
- A flip chart or lining paper and marker pens
- Bread and butter to pass round; large bloomer loaf; small pitta bread
- An egg timer
- Two copies of list as specified
- Items for prayer tables:
  - four bread baskets
  - small bread roll, paper hearts
  - family loaf, finger puppets or paper people
  - bloomer loaf, gold confetti crosses
- Mini-rolls or mini-muffins (optional)
- Mini-scripts for prayer hosts (see pp. 79–80)

WE GATHER

Opening hymn

Formal introduction

Minister The Lord be with you.

All **And also with you.**

Informal welcome

Minister Today is all about Jesus! Of course, all our worship is all about Jesus, but today we will be thinking especially about who we think Jesus is and who he came to help.

The following words have a strong rhythm and could be accompanied by a drum beat, using an African-style drum. On the word 'We' invite people to punch the air.

Voice It's good to praise your name, God of love.

All **We praise your name!**

Minister It's good to be here, God of love.

All **We praise your name!**

Minister It's good to know you, God of love.

All **We praise your name!**

Minister It's good you love us all, God of love.

All **We praise your name!**

We say sorry

Minister Sometimes we forget to do what God or others ask us to do, sometimes on purpose, sometimes in weakness. So we are going to be still for a moment and say sorry to God and ask for his forgiveness.

(Invite people to clasp hands together tightly as if holding something.)

Voice 1   God, we are sorry that we are mean and selfish. We forget to share everything that is good in our lives. Hear us.

All   **And forgive us.**

(Invite people to cross hands over their bodies, touching shoulders.)

Voice 2   God, we are sorry because we are unkind and uncaring. We don't trust you or ourselves, and we ignore the good news of your love. Hear us.

All   **And forgive us.**

(Invite people to place hands on knees and keep heads low.)

Voice 1   God, we are sorry that we are lazy and thoughtless. We don't look up to you or out to your world. Hear us.

All   **And forgive us.**

Minister   Almighty God,
who in Jesus Christ has given us
a kingdom that cannot be destroyed,
forgive *us our* sins,
open *our* eyes to God's truth,
strengthen *us* to do God's will
and give *us* the joy of his kingdom,
through Jesus Christ our Lord.

All   **Amen.**[1]

Hymn/Gloria

Collect or prayer for the day

See note in Chapter 6, How to use the service outlines.

Minister   God of constant mercy,
who sent your Son to save us:
remind us of your goodness,
increase your grace within us,
that our thankfulness may grow,
through Jesus Christ our Lord.
Amen.[2]

 WE LISTEN

Reading(s)

Old Testament reading/first reading

If you are using more than one reading, use contemporary versions for the Old Testament or Epistle.

Gospel reading/second reading

As this is a really well-known story, introduce the reading by discussion, asking the congregation to tell you what they know about this story. Simply accept all the suggestions, writing them up on a large sheet of paper (flip chart/ or lining paper).

Alternatively you might like to have a quiz about the story (see Additional resource: August on p. 81 for ideas).

Then at the end of the discussion get someone to read from Matthew's Gospel.

Talk

Before beginning the talk, start passing round a couple of plates of bread and butter. Simply take a bit yourself, then encourage the first person to try some. Ignore the circulating plates for most of the time, checking occasionally that people are enjoying the bread and butter.

Split the congregation into two 'sides' or teams. Appoint leaders who come out to the front and stand in front of their teams. (The leaders must be old enough to read and listen well.)

Hold up an egg timer. Explain that each team leader has a list of ten amazing things that Jesus did. When the time starts each team has two minutes to guess the ten things on the list – they have to guess exactly! The winner is the team that gets the most correct answers. The list might include bless children/heal lepers/walk on water/raise girl from the dead/feed 5,000/calm the storm/forgive sins/talk to a woman/make a blind man see/rise from the dead.

Say something similar to:

Jesus did many amazing things in his life, things that made people talk and wonder. All the time people were asking: 'Who is he? What kind of person does these things?'

Ask people to imagine how they would have felt if they had been at the feeding of the five thousand.

People had gone because they were curious and now they were even more curious.
Jesus had fed so many people. In John's Gospel this miracle is followed by lots of teaching. Jesus says,

'I am the bread of life' – which is a strange answer to the question: 'Who is he?'

(*Hold up a huge bloomer loaf.*) I wonder if this is the kind of bread that is Jesus. Consider how many people this loaf might feed.

Or maybe Jesus is more like this. (*Hold up a small pitta bread.*)

Talk about which kind of bread might be like Jesus.

> Jesus fed five thousand people – not counting women and children.

Consider having a side discussion about how many more that would have been.

> The exact number doesn't really matter. There would have been enough for everyone. Jesus can meet the needs of the whole world. (*Hold out the large loaf again.*)

> But (*hold out the small pitta*) Jesus also meets the needs of each individual person.

Talk about the bread and butter that's going round the congregation – ask if everyone has had a chance to enjoy it. Perhaps some people passed it on without tasting; some might have refused; some might have thought it was weird!

> Jesus not only provided bread . . . Jesus is bread. Jesus is a gift for everyone – but we have to get involved, to take Jesus at his word and believe that he is for everyone.

 WE RESPOND

Creed or statement of faith

Making connections

Minister   We've thought about how Jesus is for every person. Let's remind ourselves of how we all belong together as we say:

All   **Though he was divine,**
he did not cling to equality with God,
but made himself nothing.
Taking the form of a slave,
he was born in human likeness.
He humbled himself
and was obedient to death,
even the death of the cross.
Therefore God has raised him on high,
and given him the name above every name:

that at the name of Jesus
every knee should bow,
and every voice proclaim that Jesus Christ
   is Lord,
to the glory of God the Father.
Amen.[3]

Prayers

Create four prayer tables, set as if for a meal and including a bread basket, around the church, as below. Each table needs a host.

The congregation moves to the stations in small groups.

Table 1: empty bread basket

As people approach, the host says: 'Welcome to my table. Here there is nothing, no bread, no milk, nothing to share. Take a few moments to stand quietly and think of those who have little or nothing today. Pray for those who are in governments making decisions about caring for others, and pray for peace.'

Table 2: small bread roll; bowl of paper hearts

As people approach, the host says: 'Welcome to my table. Here there is just enough for one person, maybe a little to share. Remember that Jesus' love reaches to everyone and take time to pray for one person today, perhaps someone you know or for yourself, asking Jesus to come and meet your needs.'

Invite people to take a paper heart and place it on the table as a sign of the prayer.

Table 3: family loaf; basket of mini-finger puppets or paper people

As people approach, the host says: 'Welcome to my table. Here there is enough to feed a family, with some for visitors. Walk around the table, remember your family and friends, and pray for the places where you meet others – school, work, shops, play. Pray that homes will be places of love and sharing, and that we will be people who share Jesus with others.'

Invite people to place a puppet or paper person round the plate.

Table 4: bloomer loaf; bowl of gold confetti crosses

As people approach, the host says: 'Welcome to my table. Here there is enough to feed a crowd, enough for a feast. Gather round the table, remember that Jesus meets the needs of the world, and Jesus' love is for everyone. Pray for this church as we gather together around Jesus and share bread together, that we might be a church who shares Jesus with everyone.'

Invite people to scatter the gold crosses as a sign of their prayer.

When everyone returns to their seat, gather all the prayers together in these or similar words:

Loving God, you listen to our words and to our hearts.
Hear our prayers today,
in Jesus' name.
Amen.

OR

If your church is not able or ready to create stations, then invite the table hosts to stand at the front holding a plate as indicated in each section. Then introduce in the same way, keeping silence after each section.

If the service is a service of the word, it may be appropriate to end the prayers with the Lord's Prayer, before sharing the peace together. If the service is a Eucharist, continue with the peace followed by bringing of gifts, preparing the table and the eucharistic prayer. Involve different generations as appropriate.

The peace

Introduce the peace, using these or similar words:

Minister	God makes peace within us – let us claim it. God makes peace between us – let us share it. The peace of the Lord be with you.
All	**And also with you.**[4]

 # WE GO OUT

Notices may be included at this point as part of moving the focus to our Christian lives.

If you are able you might like to give everyone a mini-loaf or mini-muffin as a reminder that Jesus is the bread of life – for everyone.

Blessing

Minister	God's love is shown in Jesus for you and for me (*point to someone else and to self*). God's love is shown in Jesus for those we love (*stretch hands out a short distance from body and turn towards those around*). God's love is shown in Jesus for the whole world (*make large expansive gesture*). And the blessing of God, Creator, Redeemer, Sustainer, be with you and those you love, this day and always. Amen.

Notes

1 *New Patterns for Worship*, London: Church House Publishing, 2008, p. 97, B81. Copyright © Bryan Spinks and reproduced by kind permission.
2 *Common Worship: Additional Collects*, London: Church House Publishing, 2004, p. 22.
3 *New Patterns for Worship*, p. 165, E9.
4 *New Women Included*, London: SPCK, 1996, p. 55.

Quiz questions for Gospel reading

1   What time of day was it when the disciples wanted to move on? *evening*
2   Who was supposed to find the people something to eat? *disciples*
3   How many loaves did they have? *five*
4   In which Gospel does someone offer to share what they have? *John*
5   What did Jesus tell them to do with the loaves and the fish? *bring them to him*
6   Where did Jesus look? *up to heaven*
7   What did Jesus do to the bread? *blessed it and broke it*
8   Who gave the bread to the crowd? *the disciples*
9   How many baskets of leftovers were there? *12*
10 How many people were fed that day? *we don't know!! Five thousand men plus women and children*

Joy for everyone

September is a season of new beginnings, perhaps even more so than January. People get ready to start new things, children go back to school, and as daylight shortens so the mood changes. The lectionary brings us stories to challenge and stories of celebration – which are fitting themes for those facing change. Underlying all the instructions and warnings is an insistent message that reminds us that each of us can hold on to the joy of knowing that everyone is special, everyone matters to God.

Key lectionary readings

Please see note in Chapter 6, How to use the service outlines.

Genesis 50.15–21 'It all works out for the best'

Philippians 2.1–13 'Jesus our example'

Mark 9.30–37 'The little ones are the big ones'

You will need

- Enough multi-coloured prayer triangles cut from a sheet of A4, to be handed out as people arrive. Attach instructions to one side of the triangle, inviting people to write, draw or simply think about the things for which they want to thank God
- A washing line, clothes pegs
- Tear-shapes (e.g. rose petals) and a large box with a lid (if you can't find tear-shapes, use clean pebbles)
- A projector with images, or pictures, of tiny creatures
- Baskets of paper hearts

 WE GATHER

Opening hymn

Formal introduction

Minister The Lord be with you.

All **And also with you.**

Informal welcome

Minister September is a season of new beginnings and new challenges, and today we are going to give thanks to God for all that is good, and find a secret that will help us in every situation.

Invite everyone to take a few minutes to finish writing or drawing on a prayer flag something that they want to thank God for today. Explain that it's okay simply to think about it if you don't want to draw or write – but the flag still counts.

While a praise song is sung (e.g. 'Praise him on the trumpet') invite people to come forward and attach their flags to the washing line. (You will need a few adults to supervise this to help keep things moving along.)

When all the flags are attached, invite everyone to join in a mighty praise shout. If people wish they can also start in a crouching position and then stretch upwards as they get louder:

All Thank you, God, thank you, God! *(Repeat, getting louder, ending with a huge shout.)*[1]

We say sorry

Making connections

Minister	When we go through times of change, there are often things we regret. We might look back over the summer, or the past school year and remember the times things went wrong. We want to bring our disappointment and our sadness over the mistakes we have made to God and ask him to forgive us and help us. (*Invite everyone to come forward and place a tear-shape into a large box. NB: Rose petals are tear-shaped.*) The tear-shape reminds us of times of sadness, perhaps because we have hurt other people or because others have hurt us. Play music, e.g. Beth Neilsen Chapman, 'Hallelujah'. When everyone has placed their petals, close the lid of the box.
Voice	God promises that he keeps all our tears in a bottle. God also promises that our sins will be gone as the mist dissolves in the morning sun. God forgives and gives us the joy of a new beginning . . .
All	**Father,** **we have sinned against heaven and against you.** **We are not worthy to be called your children.** **We turn to you again.** **Have mercy on us,** **bring us back to yourself** **as those who once were dead** **but now have life through Christ our Lord.** **Amen.**[2]
Minister	Almighty God, who in Jesus Christ has given us a kingdom that cannot be destroyed, forgive *us our* sins, open *our* eyes to God's truth, strengthen *us* to do God's will and give *us* the joy of his kingdom, through Jesus Christ our Lord.
All	**Amen.**[3]

Hymn/Gloria

Collect or prayer for the day

See note in Chapter 6, How to use the service outlines.

Minister	Faithful God, who is with us at our beginnings and present in every moment, fill our hearts with joy this day as we remember again your love shown to us in Jesus, Your Son, our Saviour. Amen.

 # WE LISTEN

Reading(s)

Old Testament reading/first reading

If you are using the Old Testament story of Joseph read (or listen to) the *Big Bible Story Book* version.

Gospel reading/second reading

See Additional resource: September on p. 86 for dialogue.

Talk

You might like to project or pass round some pictures of very tiny creatures, the kind that might be living unnoticed in the church and the churchyard. If time allows, you might even send some people out to look for them. Say something similar to:

These tiny things are an important part of the ecology of our world, and yet most of the time we ignore them. Big animals like elephants and lions and, yes, humans, can seem so much more exciting and important.

Our world has a funny view of importance: we think that people like the headteacher are more important than the cleaner, or that the vicar is more important than the flower arrangers. When we go to a new school, it's easy to think that the bigger children are more important, and more valuable than we are, especially when we are physically small as well.

Jesus' disciples thought like this as well. They were always arguing about who was important in God's kingdom. They wanted to sit in the best seats and have the most power. But Jesus thought differently. And when he wanted to teach them about who is special in God's eyes he chose something very small. Not as small as a mini-beast, but something that was very unimportant in the world Jesus lived in. Jesus chose a child.

He took a small person and placed her right in the middle of all the arguing grown-ups.

Can you imagine it?

Wonder together about how the child felt, and how the disciples felt.

Then Jesus said that the person who wants to be first must be a servant. And he said that even small children were to be welcomed as if they were Jesus himself!

Jesus' whole life was about saying that people matter – and especially those who others think don't count.

It's an amazing thing: whoever we are, whatever we do, we are special and important to God. Every morning we can look in the mirror and say to ourselves: I am important to God. It's a secret joy, and when we are filled with joy, then we can share that with others. We can live our lives helping others discover the same thing, just as Jesus did.

 WE RESPOND

Creed or statement of faith

Making connections

Minister	Let's declare together all that we believe, filled with joy that God loves each one of us:
All	**We believe in God the Father, from whom every family in heaven and on earth is named.**
	We believe in God the Son, who lives in our hearts through faith, and fills us with his love.
	We believe in God the Holy Spirit, who strengthens us with power from on high.
	We believe in one God; Father Son and Holy Spirit. Amen.[4]

Prayers

The response to 'We pray to you, Lord' is 'Hear us', accompanied by a double hand clap.

Add in as many petitions as you wish; each petition can be offered by a different person.

Voice	Lord God, you are holy Lord God, you are good Lord God, you are holy We pray to you, Lord.
All	**Hear us.**
Voice	For those living in dangerous situations, of war, injustice or poverty . . . we pray to you, Lord.
	For those struggling with fear and anxiety . . . we pray to you, Lord. For those who are unwell . . . we pray to you, Lord. For those who miss someone they love . . . we pray to you, Lord. For those who have been hurt by someone else . . . we pray to you, Lord. For our playgroups and schools . . . we pray to you, Lord. For our teachers and helpers and all who are with us each day . . . we pray to you, Lord. For our friends and families, near or far away . . . we pray to you, Lord. For our church and its leaders, here in this place and across the world . . . we pray to you, Lord. For ourselves as we follow Jesus each day . . . we pray to you, Lord.

If the service is a service of the word, it may be appropriate to end the prayers with the Lord's Prayer, before sharing the peace together. If the service is a Eucharist, continue with the peace followed by the bringing of gifts, the preparing of the table and the eucharistic prayer. Involve different generations as appropriate.

The peace

Introduce the peace, using these or similar words:

Minister	Jesus said: 'Love one another. As I have loved you, so you are to love one another.'[5] The peace of the Lord be with you.
All	**And also with you.**

➡ WE GO OUT

Notices may be included at this point as part of moving the focus to our Christian lives.

As part of the dismissal invite some people, a mix of all ages, to come forward and collect baskets of paper hearts. Hand them round with the words: 'Take this and remember you are special to God.'

Blessing

Minister   May the joy of the Lord keep your heart singing
and your feet dancing
in your work and in your play, in your staying in
and in your going out.
And the blessing of God,
Father, Son and Holy Spirit,
be with you and those you love
this day and always.
Amen.

Notes

1 Sandra Millar, *Resourcing Summer*, Gloucester: Jumping Fish, 2009, p. 27.
2 *New Patterns for Worship*, London: Church House Publishing, 2008, p. 88, B52.
3 *New Patterns for Worship*, p. 97, B81. Copyright © Bryan Spinks and reproduced by kind permission.
4 *New Patterns for Worship*, p. 166, E12.
5 *New Patterns for Worship*, p. 276, H33.

You will need a minimum of four adults and one child.

One adult is Jesus; the others crowd around him as he walks down the church.

The child should be sitting quietly on a step or chair.

Narrator Jesus and the disciples were walking and talking, talking and walking, as they made their way through Galilee. The disciples huddled around Jesus, trying to keep the talking as quiet as possible. Jesus was telling them difficult things.

Jesus It's difficult. It's hard for you to understand. But things are changing. There is going to be betrayal, there is going to be death and there is going to be new life again.

Disciples *(muttering)* What's he on about? Do you understand?

One disciple *(loudly)* But I want to know where I fit in with all this!

  (*Disciples begin to argue and push one another.*)

Narrator Jesus and the disciples arrived at the house in Capernaum.

Jesus Come on now. What were you lot arguing about? Don't tell me it was nothing.

Narrator But the disciples said nothing. They looked out the window. They looked at the floor. They looked at the ceiling. And said nothing. They had been arguing about who was the most important of them.

  (*Jesus walks over and sits next to the child, putting his arm around her.*)

Jesus If you want to be first, then you must be the servant of everyone. Everyone. Whether important or ignored. If you welcome a child like this in my name, you are welcoming me.

Narrator The disciples were still silent.

October

Time for everyone

October marks a real change in the seasons. Autumn has a special beauty and the changing colours and landscape can make us particularly aware of time. It is often a challenge in the life of Christian discipleship to stay with the moment, to persist and be faithful in a place or with an action, so this outline picks up lectionary themes about time and patience. It centres on a story from the Old Testament, which provides great examples of God's faithfulness and human character.

Key lectionary readings

Please see note in Chapter 6, How to use the service outlines.

2 Kings 5.1–19 'The right time for the right action'

2 Timothy 3.14—4.5 'Carry on carrying on'

Luke 18.1–8 'Pray and pray some more'

You will need

- A large alarm clock
- A large calendar
- A video clip of a false start to a race (optional)
- Symbols to represent each of the seasons

 WE GATHER

Opening hymn

Formal introduction

Minister   The Lord be with you.

All   And also with you.

Informal welcome

Minister   Today we are thinking about time – and right now it's time to give God praise and thanks. Imagine that the church is a giant clock, and you are standing in it facing the altar, which is 12.

(Everyone takes a quarter-turn clockwise (which will be to the right; left from the point of view of a minister between the altar and the congregation)).

Voice   It's time to gather as God's people.

All   It's time for God.

(Everyone makes quarter-turn, towards the back.)

Voice   It's time to listen as God's people.

All   it's time for God.

(Everyone makes a further quarter-turn.)

Voice   It's time to pray as God's people.

All   It's time for God.

(Everyone makes a quarter-turn to the front.)

Voice   It's time to celebrate as God's people.

All   It's time for God.

(As everyone is facing the front again say together:)
It's time!

We say sorry

Making connections

Voice   For everything there is a season and a time for every matter under heaven.

Minister   There is a time to rejoice and be glad and a time to repent and be sorry.

(Place a large alarm clock visibly at the front.)

In the stillness we will remember the times we have forgotten that we are followers of Jesus.

(Set an alarm for one minute. When the alarm sounds:)

Voice	For the times when we have been too busy to help other people, forgive us.
All	**Lord, have mercy.**
Voice	For the times when we have been too lazy to do the things you ask of us, forgive us.
All	**Lord, have mercy.**
Voice	For the times when we have chosen to do things that hurt or harm, forgive us.
All	**Lord, have mercy.**
Minister	May the God of love bring *us* back to himself, forgive *us our* sins, and assure *us* of his eternal love in Jesus Christ our Lord.
All	**Amen.**[1]

Hymn/Gloria

Prayer for the day

Minister	Eternal God, ruler of the planets and the seasons, who speaks to every generation, speak to us today, and call us to follow you and see your kingdom come, in Jesus' name. Amen.

 **WE LISTEN**

Reading(s)

Old Testament reading

As the Old Testament reading is the key reading, see Additional resource: October on p. 91 for story version with participation.

Talk

Say something similar to:

Time was ticking away for Naaman. Every day meant his horrible skin disease was getting worse. Or at least not getting any better. It didn't matter what he did, how much time he rested or how much time he worked, nothing was changing.

(Hold up clock.) As the hours went round – get up, eat lunch, work hard, talk to family, sleep – so did Naaman's life.

Ask people how the days pass for them: are they busy, or slow?

(Hold up calendar.) And as the hours passed, so did the days and the weeks. Special days came and went but not the day when the disease disappeared.

Ask people about things marked on their calendars as special days.

But then Naaman's serving girl decided it was time to speak. She told him about the prophet who could help him, and he wondered if it was time for things to change. But when Naaman met the prophet Elisha, he thought he could buy his way to time. But Elisha knew that there is a time for everything – and God's time is not always our time.

Ask people what they think of the phrase: 'It happened at the right time' or the opposite.

This kind of time is nothing to do with calendars or clocks . . . but is to do with the sense that everything is in place ready for something to happen. Sometimes we get impatient and try to do things ahead of time. Think about a runner on the starting blocks going before the gun. It's called a false start. *(If possible, show a clip from a sports event.)*

(Show the clock and calendar again.) Naaman wanted things to happen quickly. But Elisha made him take his time. He had to bathe not once, not twice, but seven times in the river . . . and then he was healed! The time had come . . . and Naaman found it was time to believe in God.

It's not always easy to keep going when we want things to change. It's not easy to keep working towards something when the result seems so far away – or as if it's never going to happen. God looks at time differently from the way we experience it – we might say that God takes the long view. Jesus encourages us to be persistent in prayer, to keep on doing the things we should be doing – reading God's word, telling people about Jesus, helping those in need. And in the middle of the ordinary moments of the day, there will be special times when we know that God is at work, changing things and helping us to be changed.

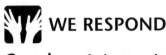 WE RESPOND

Creed or statement

Making connections

Minister   It's time to declare together all that we believe, trusting in God who is with us in every time and every place.

All   **We believe in God the Father,
God almighty, by whose plan
earth and heaven sprang to being,
all created things began.
We believe in Christ the Saviour,
Son of God in human frame,
virgin-born, the child of Mary
upon whom the Spirit came.**

         **Christ, who on the cross forsaken,
like a lamb to slaughter led,
suffered under Pontius Pilate,
he descended to the dead.
We believe in Jesus risen,
heaven's king to rule and reign,
to the Father's side ascended
till as judge he comes again.**

         **We believe in God the Spirit;
in one Church, below, above:
saints of God in one communion,
one in holiness and love.
So by faith, our sins forgiven,
Christ our Saviour, Lord and friend,
we shall rise with him in glory
to the life that knows no end.**[2]

(*May be sung to any 87.87 or 87.87.D tune.*)

Prayers

The seasons of the year

Show a picture or symbol of spring, e.g. daffodils and buds.

Voice   This is the time of new beginnings, of energy and joy.
Lord God, we thank you for the gift of each new day, and the good things that bring us delight. We pray for those who are celebrating today, whether birthdays or anniversaries. We pray for all those who long to make a new start, that you would give them courage and vision to begin. We pray for all those who are in need of joy and energy, and ask that you would give them vision and hope.
Lord, hear our prayer,

All   **Please.**

         (*Show a picture or symbol of summer, e.g. green fields, holiday scenes.*)

Voice   This is the time of growing and playing, learning and laughing.
Lord God, we thank you for all the places where we live out our lives, discovering more of your world. We pray for those who teach others, and those who work to bring health and healing. We pray for those who work with creation, as farmers or researchers, and we pray for those places where life is difficult, especially remembering . . .
Lord, hear our prayer,

All   **Please.**

         (*Show a symbol or picture of autumn, e.g. trees changing colour, acorns, harvest.*)

Voice   This is the time of changing, of night drawing in, of harvests gathered.
Lord God, we know that you are always with us. We pray for those who are going through times of difficulty, and for those who will be with them. We remember especially . . . and ask that you would be close to them through this time.
Lord, hear our prayer,

All   **Please.**

         (*Show a picture or symbol of winter, e.g. snow, Christmas, frozen lakes.*)

Voice   This is the season of waiting and patience, of faithfulness and hope.
Lord God, we thank you for those who are passionate to see change in our world, who work for justice and speak out for peace. We pray for all who campaign on behalf of others, especially for the work of . . . We pray for those who are struggling in relationships and those who work to bring about reconciliation.
Lord, hear our prayer,

All   **Please.**

         (*Show all four pictures together.*)

Voice   Lord God, we thank you for your love which is always present, like a golden thread holding everything together. We pray for the Church as we try to share that love with others, and ask that you would help us to carry on following you all the days of our lives.
Lord, hear our prayer,

All   **Please.**

Voice   Lord God, accept our prayers today, in Jesus' name.
Amen.

If the service is a service of the word, it may be appropriate to end the prayers with the Lord's Prayer, before sharing the peace together. If the service is a Eucharist, continue with the peace followed by the bringing of gifts, the preparing of the table and the eucharistic prayer. Involve different generations as appropriate.

The peace

Introduce the peace, using these or similar words:

Minister   God has called us to live in peace.
             The peace of the Lord be always with you.

All   **And also with you.**[3]

 **WE GO OUT**

Notices may be included at this point as part of moving the focus to our Christian lives.

Invite people to tap their wrists where a watch usually sits.

Voice   God is good, all the time.
          All the time, God is good.

All   **God is good, all the time.**
          All the time, God is good.

Encourage people to repeat this during the week ahead.

Blessing

Voice   For everything there is a season and a time for
            every matter under heaven.

Minister We go into the world
            with time to share God's love
            and time to know God's presence.
            And the blessing of God,
            Creator, Redeemer and Sustainer
            be with you and those you love
            this day and always.
            Amen.

Notes

1 *New Patterns for Worship*, London: Church House Publishing, 2008, p. 95, B73. Copyright © Stuart Thomas and reproduced by kind permission.
2 *New Patterns for Worship*, p. 164, E8.
3 *New Patterns for Worship*, p. 272, H2.

The story of Naaman

Actions

These actions are to be done every time this person or situation is mentioned in the telling of the story:

- Captain in the army   (*Hand to head in salute.*) Yes, sir!
- Little serving girl   (*Lower hand.*) Aaah!
- Horrible skin disease   (*Shake hand as if dirty.*) Ugh!
- Man of God   (*Place hands together as if in prayer.*)
- The one true God   (*Raise forefinger slowly towards heaven.*)

In one of the countries next door to Israel, there was a great man and an important captain in the army. His name was Naaman. Now life is pretty good when you are an important captain in the army. Everything was going well for Naaman. Many battles had been won and many prizes had been taken. Only one thing spoiled his life. And it wasn't a small thing either. It was a terrible thing for an important captain in the army. For Naaman had a horrible skin disease, a really horrible skin disease . . . and there was nothing he could do about it.

But during one of his many battles with Israel he had captured a little serving girl who now worked for the important captain's important wife. She heard all about the horrible skin disease and remembered the man of God in her home country. The little serving girl was scared to speak to the wife of the important captain in the army. But one day she decided it was time. So the little serving girl told the wife of the captain in the army about the man of God who could heal the horrible skin disease.

So Naaman set off to find the man of God, whose name was Elisha.

When the important captain in the army arrived at the house of the man of God, he sent him a message asking him to heal his horrible skin disease. The man of God sent a message back. He said: 'Tell the important captain in the army that he must bathe in the River Jordan not once, not twice, but seven times, and then he will be healed of the horrible skin disease.'

Now the important captain in the army was very disappointed at this. He thought that he was so important that the man of God would come out in person and wave his arm about and heal him. Surely the rivers in his own country were more than good enough even for an important captain in the army! He ranted and raved, and raved and ranted. Finally, a servant (not the little serving girl, you realize) interrupted and said: 'If the man of God had asked you to do something really, really, really difficult, you would have done it willingly. So why don't you just get on with doing something easy, like washing in a river?' (He was a very brave servant to interrupt the important captain in the army!)

So Naaman went down to the river. He went into the water not once, not twice, but seven times. And on the seventh time the important captain in the army looked down and realized that the horrible skin disease had disappeared. He was healed!

Together with all his followers, the important captain in the army went back to the man of God and said: 'Now I know that there is only one true God in all the earth and I will serve him always.'

The man of God said simply: 'Go in peace.'

And the important captain in the army went home, healed of his horrible skin disease.

I bet the little serving girl was pleased!

Invitation for everyone

By November we become very aware of the changing focus of the church year. This season is sometimes called the kingdom season, as the lectionary focuses on the kingdom drawing close, on the vision of a heavenly banquet and of judgement. The month begins with All Saints' and All Souls' and moves towards the feast of Christ the King. This outline uses key readings which pick up the theme of invitation and acceptance, of behaviour and belonging.

Key lectionary readings

Please see note in Chapter 6, How to use the service outlines.

Isaiah 25.6–9 'A feast for everyone'

2 Thessalonians 2.1–5, 13–15 'Watch for the day'

Matthew 25.31–46 'Living like sheep'

You will need

- Party clothes, e.g. shoes, jewellery, hair clips; some cards with rules for behaving at parties
- Lining paper; lots of gold-coloured discs OR five large candles
- An invitation card for each person

 ## WE GATHER

Opening hymn

Formal introduction

Minister   The Lord be with you.

All   **And also with you.**

Informal welcome

Minister   Today we are turning towards Advent, thinking about heaven, eternity and the kingdom of God. We remember that God has invited everyone to the great heavenly banquet!

Voice   The people of God are in every place.

Echo   Every place, every place, every place.

Voice   The saints of God are in every time.

Echo   Every time, every time, every time.

Voice   The followers of God are in every age.

Echo   Every age, every age, every age . . .

Voice   In every place, every time, every age, we worship today.

Echo   We worship, we worship, we worship . . .

Voice   (shouts) Today!

All   **Today!**

We say sorry

Making connections

Minister   The invitation has gone out to all people to the great heavenly banquet, but sometimes we ignore the invitation and sometimes we forget what we should do.
In the stillness, we each remember all the times we have let ourselves down, ignored other people, and forgotten God.

(Invite everyone to stand.)

Voice   Lord God, forgive us for acting as if we were in charge of things, and forgetting that you have called us.
Lord, have mercy.

All   **Lord, have mercy.**

(Invite everyone to sit.)

Voice   Lord God, forgive us for thinking that we are not good enough to come to your feast.

Christ, have mercy.

All **Christ, have mercy.**

(*Invite everyone to kneel.*)

Voice Lord God, forgive us for forgetting to come to you in prayer and praise.
Lord, have mercy.

All **Lord, have mercy.**

(*Invite everyone to put their heads in their hands.*)

Voice Lord God, forgive us for not looking and listening to the needs of your world.
Christ, have mercy.

All **Christ, have mercy.**

(*Invite everyone to stand.*)

Minister But hear the word of God in Jesus Christ!
We are forgiven people!
May the God of love and power
forgive *you* and free *you* from *your* sins,
heal and strengthen *you* by his Spirit,
and raise *you* to new life in Christ our Lord.[1]

Hymn/Gloria

Prayer for the day

Minister Almighty God,
who has made a feast for all the nations
and promised to wipe away every tear,
strengthen each one of us to live our lives
as redeemed and chosen people,
worthy of our calling,
and joyful in our hope,
through Jesus Christ our Lord
Amen.

 **WE LISTEN**

Reading(s)

Old Testament reading/first reading

The Isaiah reading could be from a scroll, proclaiming it from a high point.

If the technology allows, it could be accompanied by visual images of banquets and rich food.

Gospel reading/second reading

There are various dramas and poems based on this passage including 'The sheep and the goats' from *Godspell* and *The Electric Gospel* by Peter Dainty.

Talk

Say something similar to:

> I would like to invite someone here to a party. It's a really special party . . . I wonder what would make a party special for you?

Listen to some ideas.

Refer to party scenes from films like the invisible food banquet in *Hook* or the wedding banquet in *Shrek*.

Take some time to choose a person to come to the party.

When the person is at the front, look him or her over carefully and then decide that he or she looks all wrong. Explain that this is a very posh party, the kind of party given for royal weddings. Everyone wears their best clothes (put some bling on the guest), wears their best shoes (get the person to put different shoes on), and does their hair in the best possible style (restyle hair). Say something similar to:

> Now you are ready to go. Are you still willing? It's not just any invitation, you know. These invitations are like gold dust.

> Now everyone who is going to the party not only wears their best clothes, best shoes and best hairdo, they also have to be on their best behaviour.

> Who knows what that means at a party?

Draw a few cards out with phrases like: 'Don't throw jelly'; 'Say "thank you"'; 'Admire the birthday girl'; 'Don't cry when she wins everything'; 'Eat what you're given', etc.

Throw the cards away.

> This party isn't that kind of party. It seems best behaviour is a bit different.

Pull out a different selection of cards with phrases like: 'Feed the hungry'; 'Provide water'; 'Welcome strangers'; 'Give away clothes'; 'Help the sick'; 'Visit people in prison'.

Ask the guest how many of these he or she has done, then say to the congregation:

> This is a very special party. Do you still want to go?

> This party is the party that God is preparing for the whole world.

The invitation is to everyone. Imagine a table so big everyone can sit there.

Run up and down the nave to demonstrate possibilities; include some statistics of global population, etc.

It's not very exclusive. And it doesn't matter what you look like. (*Take bling, etc., from guest.*)

It doesn't matter how old, how young, how fat or thin, how clever or stupid you are (which is just as well, looking around). Everyone is invited.

But what really matters is how you behave. Because once you know you are a guest of the King, the God of the whole universe, then things begin to change. You start to look at things differently.

Talk about how followers of Jesus work to change the world, work to help those who are neglected and forgotten discover that they are invited too.

There's a place for everyone. We're invited – now let's live like guests of the King!

 ## WE RESPOND

Creed or statement of faith

Making connections

Minister	Let's declare our faith in the God who has invited everyone to share in his kingdom. Do you believe and trust in God the Father, source of all being and life, the one for whom we exist?
All	**We believe and trust in him.**
Minister	Do you believe and trust in God the Son, who took our human nature, died for us and rose again?
All	**We believe and trust in him.**
Minister	Do you believe and trust in God the Holy Spirit, who gives life to the people of God and makes Christ known in the world?
All	**We believe and trust in him.**
Minister	This is the faith of the Church.
All	**This is our faith.** **We believe and trust in one God, Father, Son and Holy Spirit. Amen.**[2]

Prayers

Lay out a long sheet of lining paper in a place where people can access it easily.

Explain that this represents the heavenly banquet. Give everyone some gold discs to represent haloes. After each section of the prayer, pause to allow peope to come and place the discs on the banquet cloth as a sign of their prayer. (It may be appropriate to invite specific people to do this, and collect them from the congregation at the right moment.) Play Taizé music while people lay discs on the table, e.g 'O Lord, hear our prayer' or 'Grant me a place at your table'.

Use different voices for the different sections.

Play music to begin.

Voice 1	We pray for all those who have not yet heard that God loves them and has a place for them at his table and we pray that God will give courage to us as we share the good news.
Voice 2	We pray for all those who are hungry for food today and those who have no water, and for those who work for peace and justice in our world. We pray that God will give them the words to say and the actions to do.
Voice 3	We pray for all those who are without homes, without clothing and who have no one to love them, especially praying for those in prison. We pray for those who work alongside them, especially . . .
Voice 4	We pray for those who are unwell, in mind or body, and pray that those who work with them out of love or duty will be moved by compassion.
Voice 5	We pray for ourselves and ask that God will help us to use our gifts and strengths to live our lives as guests at his banquet, sharing with those in need and welcoming those who are strangers . . .
	(*When all the prayers have been said:*)
Minister	Lord God, you promised to hear us when we pray. Accept the prayers we have offered, spoken aloud or in our hearts, for Jesus' sake. Amen.

OR

If placing the 'haloes' on the table is not suitable for your context, an alternative is to have five candle bearers. Each person brings a candle forward to place on the table, and a voice offers the prayer as outlined above.

If the service is a service of the word, it might be a good idea to end the prayers with the Lord's Prayer, before sharing the peace together. If the service is a Eucharist, continue with the peace followed by the bringing of gifts, the preparing of the table and the eucharistic prayer. Involve different generations as appropriate.

The peace

Introduce the peace, using these or similar words:

Minister   God is love
and those who live in love live in God
and God lives in them.[3]
The peace of the Lord be with you.

All   **And also with you.**

 WE GO OUT

Notices may be included at this point as part of moving the focus to our Christian lives.

Hand an invitation card to people as they leave.

Blessing

Voice   So then stand firm, people of God, and be faithful.

Minister   May our generous God meet all your needs
and our loving God hold you fast.
And the blessing of God,
    Father, Son and Holy Spirit,
be with you and those you love,
this day and always.
Amen.

Notes

1 *New Patterns for Worship*, London: Church House Publishing, 2008, p. 97, B80.
2 *New Patterns for Worship*, p. 163, E6.
3 *New Patterns for Worship*, p. 272, H6.

December

Promise for everyone

December brings us to the beginning of the church year, but for the vast majority of people it brings us to Christmas. The challenge is to use the lectionary to recapture a sense of Advent, of preparing for the coming of Christ as infant and later as king. It is also about preparing our own lives, ready to welcome Jesus once again. This worship outline draws on Advent themes and readings, especially the person of John the Baptist, to explore preparation and promise.

Key lectionary readings

Please see note in Chapter 6, How to use the service outlines. If being used as a principal service in Advent, the lectionary readings for the day must be used in a Church of England service.

Isaiah 11.1–10 'The dawn of a new world'

Philippians 1.3–11 'Praying for completion'

Mark 1.1–8 'The voice in the wilderness'

You will need

- An Advent candle, matches
- A shopping bag containing
  - cards
  - decorations
  - wrapping paper
  - mince pies
- Enough Christmas decoration paper shapes with ties for everyone, e.g. star shapes, angel shapes, bauble shapes
- A small tree to hang the decorations on

WE GATHER

Opening hymn

Formal introduction

Minister The Lord be with you.

All **And also with you.**

Informal welcome

Minister We are now in the season of Advent, a time of promise and a time of preparing. We will light the Advent candle and pray that God will be with us here.
God who speaks.

All **Help us to listen.**

Minister God who listens.

All **Help us to pray.**

Minister God who sees.

All **Help us to act.**

Minister God who acts.

All **Help us to share.**
Amen.[1]

(Lighting the candle:)

Voice We are waiting, for you, O Lord. We are waiting for you.

Minister We light this candle and remember God's word spoken down the ages, a promise of peace and life for everyone.

All **Peace and life for everyone.**

Minister Let us pray:
O God of hope, send your light to us as we make ready to welcome Jesus again. Live in us and help us to live in you. Amen.

We say sorry

Making connections

Minister	Advent is a time of getting ready, getting ready in our own lives, ready to welcome Jesus once again. We come to God asking for his forgiveness for all that we have done wrong and remembering all the wrong in our world.
	(Invite people to touch and hold the appropriate fingers of their left hands as the prayers are read.)

Thumb

Voice	Lord, forgive us for forgetting that you are God and for failing to follow your ways. Lord, have mercy.
All	**Lord, have mercy.**

First finger

Voice	Lord, forgive us for pointing at faults in others and forgetting our own mistakes. Christ, have mercy.
All	**Christ, have mercy.**

Longest finger

Voice	Lord, forgive us for going our own way and ignoring your direction for our lives. Lord, have mercy.
All	**Lord, have mercy.**

Ring finger

Voice	Lord, forgive us for hurting those closest to us and for not building relationships with others. Christ, have mercy.
All	**Christ, have mercy.**

Smallest finger

Voice	Lord, forgive us for overlooking those who seem to be of no account and forgetting how special each one of us is to you. Lord, have mercy.
All	**Lord, have mercy.**
Minister	May God our Father forgive *us our* sins and bring *us* to the fellowship of his table with his saints for ever.
All	**Amen.**[2]

Hymn

Collect or prayer for the day

See note in Chapter 6, How to use the service outlines.

Minister	Faithful God, you keep your promises and come to meet us again in Jesus, help us to prepare our lives and make space for you once again through Jesus Christ our Lord Amen.

 **WE LISTEN**

Readings

Old Testament reading/first reading

Someone could read the prophecy from a scroll (see Additional resource: December on p. 100 for alternative version). If technology permits, accompany the reading with appropriate images.

Gospel reading/second reading

Someone could read 'Wild John' as an alternative Gospel (from *The Electric Bible* by Peter Dainty).

Talk

Ask a question such as:

> I wonder if anyone knows how we know Christmas is on its way?

Ask for a few ideas.

Hold up a shopping bag, and bring out some of the following – cards, decoration, wrapping paper, mince pies.

Remind people of the scene in *The Lion, the Witch and the Wardrobe*, when it was always winter but never Christmas. (If you can, show a clip from the film.)

> The biggest clue that things were changing was the arrival of Father Christmas and the presents. Sometimes it seems as if getting ready for Christmas is hard work. A lot of effort goes in behind the scenes to make a home full of family, laughter and love. There are rooms to be cleared out if we expect guests, extra cooking, hours spent shopping and wrapping.
> Nowadays it all seems to cost such a lot, but it doesn't have to be that way. There's a great scene in *Little House on the Prairie* (chapter 19).[3] A man risks danger to get presents to the children for Christmas – the presents are really tiny, but really special because of the huge effort and risk to get

them. But there is also a real sense of expectation – looking forward to a very special time, looking forward to a promise kept.

God has made a promise – he has promised that one day there will be a new kind of kingdom, the kind the prophets spoke about.

Ask people for ideas as to what that kingdom will be like . . . and how we might prepare.

We might need to say sorry, we might need to mend broken relationships, we might need to work for justice and peace, make room to welcome new people into our lives. John the Baptist knew it would be hard work. He knew there would be mess and disruption – just as there is at home when we prepare for Christmas. But he also knew it was important. It will be worth it, for God keeps his promise. So let's make ready.

WE RESPOND

Creed or statement of faith

Making connections

Minister   Let's declare our faith in the God who has promised us a Saviour and a new kind of kingdom.

All   **We believe in God the Father,**
from whom every family
in heaven and on earth is named.

We believe in God the Son,
who lives in our hearts through faith,
and fills us with his love.

We believe in God the Holy Spirit,
who strengthens us
with power from on high.

We believe in one God;
Father Son and Holy Spirit.
Amen.[4]

Prayers

Hand out paper Christmas decorations. Invite people to take a few moments to write or draw or think their prayers onto their decorations, and then to come and tie the decorations to the Advent prayer tree.

While this is happening, the following is chanted by a cantor (or read aloud if no one is available to sing). After each line, pause for a few moments.

Voice   Lord God, we pray that your world will be ready for Jesus.
Lord God, we pray that our church will be ready for Jesus.
Lord God, we pray that this place will be ready for Jesus.
Lord God, we pray that our lives will be ready for Jesus.
Come Lord Jesus, Come.

When all the prayers have been tied to the tree, pray in these or similar words:

Voice   Loving God, you promise to hear us when we pray. Accept these prayers through Jesus Christ our Lord. Amen.

OR

If people cannot move easily to tie prayers to the tree, simply invite a few people to gather them up and then take time during the singing of the next hymn to tie them to the tree.

If the service is a service of the word, it might be a good idea to end the prayers with the Lord's Prayer, before sharing the peace together. If the service is a Eucharist, continue with the peace followed by the bringing of gifts, the preparing of the table and the eucharistic prayer. Involve different generations as appropriate.

The peace

Introduce the peace, using these or similar words:

Minister   May the God of peace make you completely holy, ready for the coming of our Lord Jesus Christ. The peace of the Lord be with you.

All   **And also with you.**[5]

 WE GO OUT

Notices may be included at this point as part of moving the focus to our Christian lives.

Invite everyone to say the following with actions:

Voice   Let's make our hearts ready (*make fist and tap over heart area twice*)

All   **Let's make our hearts ready** (*make fist and tap over heart area twice*)

Voice   for Jesus to be with us (*stretch both hands upwards*).

All   **For Jesus to be with us** (*stretch both hands upwards*).

Blessing

Minister   May God himself, the God of peace,
make you perfect and holy,
and keep you safe and blameless,
   in spirit, soul and body,
for the coming of our Lord Jesus Christ;
and the blessing of God, Father, Son
   and Holy Spirit,
be with you this day and always.
Amen.[6]

Notes

1 Sandra Millar, *Resourcing Easter*, Gloucester: Jumping Fish, 2008, p. 2.
2 *New Patterns for Worship*, London: Church House Publishing, 2008, p. 97, B83. Copyright © Stuart Thomas and reproduced by kind permission.
3 Laura Ingalls Wilder, *Little House on the Prairie*.
4 *New Patterns for Worship*, p. 166, E12.
5 *New Patterns for Worship*, p. 273, H12.
6 *New Patterns for Worship*, p. 305, J74.

A reading from Isaiah: A vision of a new world

A green shoot, a special person,
will come from the stump of Jesse;
from his roots a budding branch.
The Spirit of God will hover over him,
the Spirit that brings wisdom and understanding,
the Spirit that gives direction and strength,
the Spirit that instils knowledge and fear of the Lord;
he will delight in the love of God,
he won't judge by appearances,
or decide on the basis of rumour.
He will judge the needy by what is right
and make just decisions for the poor of the earth.
Then the wolf will play with the lamb,
and the leopard lie down with the kid;
the calf and the young lion will feed together,
and a little child will tend them.
The cow and the bear will be friends,
their calves and cubs grow up together;
and the lion will eat straw like the cows.
The baby will play over the rattlesnake's den,
and the toddler dance over the viper's nest.
Neither animal nor human will hurt or kill
on my holy mountain.
The whole earth will be brimming with God's love,
a living knowledge of God as the waters cover the sea.

Worship Together (London: SPCK). From Sandra Millar, *Resourcing Christmas*, Gloucester: Jumping Fish, 2007.
Copyright © Sandra Millar 2007, 2012

Recommended reading

Children's spirituality

Adams, Kate, *Unseen Worlds*, London: Jessica Kingsley, 2010.

Beckwith, Ivy, *Postmodern Children's Ministry*, Grand Rapids, Mich.: Zondervan, 2004.

Berryman, Jerome, *Children and the Theologians: Clearing the Way for Grace*, Harrisburg, Penn.: Morehouse Publishing, 2010.

Berryman, Jerome, *Godly Play: An Imaginative Approach to Religious Education*, San Francisco, Calif.: HarperSanFrancisco, 1991.

Giles, Richard, *At Heaven's Gate*, Norwich: Canterbury Press, 2010.

Morpurgo, Michael, *Singing for Mrs Pettigrew: Stories and Essays from a Writing Life*, Somerville, Mass.: Candlewick Press, 2007.

Nye, Rebecca, *Children's Spirituality: What It Is and Why It Matters*, London: Church House Publishing, 2009.

Richards, Anne and Peter Privett, *Through the Eyes of a Child*, London: Church House Publishing, 2009.

Velarde, Robert, *The Wisdom of Pixar*, Downers Grove, Ill.: IVP, 2010.

Bible and other resources

Barfield, Maggie, *The Big Bible Story Book: 188 Bible stories to Enjoy Together*, Bletchley: Scripture Union, 2007.

Book of Common Prayer

Common Worship: Additional Collects, London: Church House Publishing, 2004.

Common Worship: Daily Prayer, London: Church House Publishing, 2005.

Dainty, Peter, *The Electric Bible: Poems for Public Worship*, 2003.

Dennis, Trevor, *The Book of Books*, Oxford: Lion Hudson, 2009.

Hartman, Bob and Krisztina Kallai Nagy, *The Lion Storyteller Bible*, Oxford: Lion Hudson, 2008.

Godspell – soundtrack CD is available.

Millar, Sandra, *Resourcing Christmas*, Gloucester: Jumping Fish, 2007.

Millar, Sandra, *Resourcing Easter*, Gloucester: Jumping Fish, 2008.

Millar, Sandra, *Resourcing Summer*, Gloucester: Jumping Fish, 2009.

New Patterns for Worship, London: Church House Publishing, 2008.

The St Hilda Community, *New Women Included: A Book of Prayers and Services*, London: SPCK, 1996.